The Clinical Treatment
of the Criminal Offender
in Outpatient Mental Health Settings:
New and Emerging Perspectives

The Clinical Treatment of the Criminal Offender in Outpatient Mental Health Settings: New and Emerging Perspectives

Nathaniel J. Pallone, PhD
Sol Chaneles, PhD
Editors

The Haworth Press
New York • London

The Clinical Treatment of the Criminal Offender in Outpatient Mental Health Settings: New and Emerging Perspectives has also been published as *Journal of Offender Counseling, Services & Rehabilitation*, Volume 15, Number 1 1990.

The Haworth Press, Inc., 10 Alice Street, Binghamton, NY 13904-1580
EUROSPAN/Haworth, 3 Henrietta Street, London WC2E 8LU England

Library of Congress Cataloging-in-Publication Data

The Clinical treatment of the criminal offender in outpatient mental health settings : new and
  emerging perspectives / Nathaniel J. Pallone, Sol Chaneles, editors.
       p. cm.
       "Has also been published as Journal of offender counseling, services & rehabilitation; volume 15, number 1, 1990" — T.p. verso.
       Includes bibliographical references.
       ISBN 0-86656-982-0 (alk. paper) : $29.95
       1. Insane, Criminal and dangerous — Mental health services. 2. Psychiatric hospitals — Outpatient services. I. Pallone, Nathaniel J. II. Chaneles, Sol. [DNLM: 1. Ambulatory Care. 2. Community Mental Health Services. 3. Criminal Psychology. 4. Mental Disorders — therapy. W1 JO802R v. 15 no. 1 / WM 30 C641]
RC451.4.P68C55   1990
362.2'1 — dc20
DNLM/DLC
for Library of Congress   90-4008
                                                                                                     CIP

The Clinical Treatment of the Criminal Offender in Outpatient Mental Health Settings: New and Emerging Perspectives

CONTENTS

ABOUT THE EDITORS

Nathaniel J. Pallone, PhD, is University Distinguished Professor of clinical psychology and criminal justice, at Rutgers University, New Brunswick, New Jersey, where he previously served as dean and academic vice president. Dr. Pallone has specialized in the treatment of the "dually deviant" both in correctional and outpatient mental health settings and has been a consultant to the Connecticut Department of Corrections, the Criminal Justice Research Center in Albany, the New York State Narcotics Addiction Control Commission, and the Office of the Public Defender in New Jersey. Since 1976, he has chaired the Classification Review Board for Sex Offenders in the New Jersey Department of Corrections. Dr. Pallone is a Fellow of the American Psychological Association and the American College of Forensic Psychology and a Diplomate of the American Board of Professional Psychology. He is the author of 130 scholarly and professional articles and author or editor of eight books, the most recent of which is *Rehabilitating Criminal Sexual Psychopaths* (Transaction Books, 1990).

Sol Chaneles, PhD, was Chairman of the Department of Criminal Justice, Rutgers University, New Brunswick, New Jersey, and an elected trustee of the New Jersey Association on Correction until his untimely death in January 1990. The author of "Growing Old Behind Bars" in *Psychology Today*, September 1987, and many other articles in professional journals, Dr. Chaneles was completing a non-fiction book on art looting during World War II at the time of his death.

Introduction

Nathaniel J. Pallone

CRIMINAL OFFENDERS AND "MAINSTREAM" OUTPATIENT MENTAL HEALTH CARE: EMERGING PERSPECTIVES

It is likely folly to expect consistency in human perception and behavior in any arena, so it is not surprising that inconsistencies abound in our societal responses to criminal behavior. During the same elections in which a "Get Tough, Hang 'Em High" presidential candidate who avows wider application of the death penalty is overwhelmingly preferred over one whose posture toward prison furloughs bespeaks at least an implicit belief in the prison as an institution whose purpose is rehabilitation, and in which regional and local candidates who reveal the same "Get Tough" posture by endorsing mandatory custodial sentencing for all sorts of felony crime are similarly preferred, the same electorate declines to support the issuing of public debt bonds to support the construction of prison facilities to house those offenders who are the focus of just such policies, let alone disdaining the increased taxes required to support the staffing of those facilities.

Nor are these most recent inconsistencies singular. The same era that brought the historic *Pugh v. Locke* decision in Mr. Justice Johnson's Federal District Court in Alabama (1978), which promised to reform the prisons of the nation by requiring not only humane housing and sanitary conditions but also "meaningful programs" staffed by qualified personnel, also yielded in the Federal Congress the Kennedy-Thurmond Act of 1984, which effectively eliminated parole in the Federal prison system. A decade after *Pugh v. Locke*, dozens of states had been placed under Federal court order respecting one or another aspect of prison operation; half a decade after Kennedy-Thurmond, the Federal courts operate under constraint of a set of criminal sentencing guidelines which, by design, recapitulate the parole decision guidelines operative in the Federal prisons for the dozen years prior to enactment of the Kennedy-Thurmond legislation.

Though the number of offenses and the number of jurisdictions subject to mandatory custodial sentences increases apace, the population of the nation's prison facilities grows but modestly; nor, in the face of Federal court constraints interacting with the refusal of the taxpayer to approve construction of new facilities, could one reasonably expect otherwise. New and technologically sophisticated methods of electronic surveillance of probationers (and, in some jurisdictions, of parolees) are introduced, holding promise to relieve (whether by explicit design or by fortunate effect matters little) what would otherwise prove to be intolerable overcrowding in the prisons and jails likely to result in yet other Federal court orders. Whether by design, by happenstance, or as a sort of subliminal compensation for enacting "Get Tough" laws, other legislation (e.g., that governing the processing of alcohol and drug users in several states through pre-trial intervention programs) permits some offenders who are both formally guilty of criminal behavior *and* psychiatrically (or biochemically) disordered to be diverted from the criminal justice system into the mental health "system," even when the essential features of their disorder(s) can provide no basis for exculpation by the stringent criteria for the insanity or the "diminished responsibility" defenses, with the effect that prison populations remain relatively stable while the roster of those offenders for whom responsibility has been shifted to the mental health community rises dramatically.

There is a delicious perversity in the reading of recent social history, especially when the cast of characters remains relatively stable. Thus it is instructive to recall that it was Mr. Justice Johnson who also handed down the *Wyatt v. Hardin* and *Wyatt v. Stickney* decisions of 1971, upheld by the Supreme Court four years later in the landmark case that reformed the mental hospitals in Alabama and, by extension, of the nation, by affirming the right of patients to treatment and establishing standards to govern the ratio between patients and professional staff as well as a panoply of aspects of hospital operation. It may be even more instructive to recall that, between 1970 and 1976, as benchmarks for assessing the impact of the *Wyatt* decisions, the budget for mental hospitals in Alabama had *increased* by 230% while the patient population had *decreased* by 58%, with the "unserved" segment apparently diverted from inpatient to outpatient treatment via a network of community mental health centers not subject (or perhaps not *yet* subject) to judicially imposed standards for patient care (Pallone, 1986, pp. 33-35; Stickney, 1976).

If the judicial, legislative, and electoral arenas reveal contradictory trends, what can be said of the operational arena? Here one encounters a substantially clearer direction, perhaps readily predictable in consequence of those contradictory trends in the arenas which establish constraints and policies; and that direction is certainly a readily discernible movement away from incarceration and toward "community treatment" of one or another sort. That movement, further, appears to have occurred even in the absence of a formal (and radical) restructuring of the process of sanctioning criminal behavior of the sort proposed by von Hirsch (1985) and other proponents of the much-misunderstood "just deserts" school. Indeed, it can readily be demonstrated that formal adoption of a "just deserts" approach would likely result in imposition of more modest sentences, whether to incarceration or community supervision, than are presently yielded through an irregular, Byzantine process which aggregates charges associated with only conceptually differentiatable aspects of the same episode of criminal behavior, then permits wide-ranging plea bargains to an unrealistically magnified set of indictments, and eventuates in concurrent sentences for reduced charges.

Instead, what one observes at the clinical level is a burgeoning in the number of accused or adjudicated offenders among the roster of those served not merely in those agencies whose purpose is offender rehabilitation in the community, but also and perhaps more significantly in "mainstream" settings for outpatient mental health care, so that offenders now constitute a highly visible fraction of the patient population in community mental health centers, substance abuse rehabilitation settings, social service agencies, and even private practice. As if to reflect such a trend at the clinical level, there has been an increase between 1981-86 on the order of 400% in the number of articles in "mainstream" professional journals in psychiatry, psychology, and clinical social work which deal with issues related to the treatment of offenders. Unfortunately, no data base of national scope has yet been established to yield information about the aggregate total of offenders so served; about whether their involvement in outpatient treatment represents an act of volition, a formal diversion from criminal justice processing, a condition of probation, or a means to optimize community re-entry following parole; or about the range of formal diagnoses for which outpatient mental health treatment is sought and the putative relationship between such disorders and the criminal behavior of which offenders in outpatient treatment have been accused or convicted.

It is characteristic of outpatient mental health treatment (as indeed of clinical medicine; witness Legionnaire's disease or AIDS) that services are first provided to "new constituents" and only later are conceptual models developed which specify the ways in which such "new" constituents resemble or differ from "traditional" constituents and/or the ways in which traditional methods of treatment can or should be modified, or new methods of treatment developed, to meet the needs of "new" constituents; in this, as in much else we do, it may be appropriate that service leads and well-considered rationalization follows. Granted that we have developed a reasonable body of knowledge to guide professional intervention, for example, in the case of the depressive who occasionally undergoes a manic episode, with the mania expressed in a free-fall shopping spree which drives the Visa card balance heaven-ward, can we make the assumption that the same intervention strategies will yield positive results if the manic behavior results in assaultive behavior against a store clerk who bears the sad news that Visa's computer has declined further purchases? Or that those intervention strategies which have proved effective in treating "Sneaky Pete" alcoholics who cadge money from relatives and friends will avail when the resources to support the habit are garnered from burglary? Given the views of such neuropsychiatrists as Robert Wettstein (1987), who appears to believe that, whatever else may be true of the violent offender, it is very nearly universally the case that such offenders display neuropsychological anomalies "of sub-clinical etiology," no less than the wide overlap between substance abuse and criminal behavior, it also seems apparent that clinical neuropsychology and psychopharmacology will perforce be called upon to contribute their special expertise to the development of treatment regimens and paradigms specifically honed to the "dually deviant" offender.

Not surprisingly, the addition of offenders to the roster of those served in outpatient mental health settings has proceeded largely in the absence of differentiated conceptual models. The "first words" are now being spoken; we shall doubtless wait decades before we are able to utter "last words." The papers in this volume thus represent a contribution to the gathering of "first words" in the emerging, profession-wide, effort to gain new, appropriate, and useful perspectives on the clinical treatment of the criminal offender in outpatient mental health and social service settings. Together, they suggest both the parameters and richness of the discussion and quite pointedly signal the intersection between the "traditional" interests of the community of corrections professionals and the outpatient mental health care community, particularly in domestic violence and alcohol and substance abuse.

REFERENCES

Pallone, Nathaniel J. *On the Social Utility of Psychopathology*. New Brunswick: Transaction Books, 1986.

Stickney, Stonewall B. *"Wyatt v. Stickney*: Background and Post-Mortem," in Stuart Golann and William J. Fremouw, eds. *The Right to Treatment for Mental Patients*. New York: Irvington, 1976. Pp. 29-46.

von Hirsch, Andrew. *Past or Future Crimes: Deservedness and Dangerousness in the Sentencing of Criminals*. New Brunswick: Rutgers University Press, 1985.

Wettstein, Robert M. "Legal Aspects of Neuropsychiatry," in Robert E. Hales and Stuart C. Yudofsky, *The American Psychiatric Press Textbook of Neuropsychiatry*. Washington: American Psychiatric Association, 1987. Pp. 451-463.

"Privatizing" the Treatment of Criminal Offenders

Harold W. Demone, Jr.
Margaret Gibelman

INTRODUCTION

In the ongoing debate about the respective roles and responsibilities of the public and private sectors, there are certain "indisputable" public arenas. These concern powers bequeathed by the Constitution specifically to the federal government or reserved to the states. (Local government has no constitutional authority. Its powers are derived from the states.) One example of a purely public function is the federal government's exclusive power to provide for the nation's defense. Although not as explicit, it would be reasonable to assume that ensuring public safety is a logical extension of this governmental power.

Protecting our lives, boarders, and property from real or potential threats from sources outside the United States and protecting the citizenry against the acts of individuals or groups within our society are generally acceptable public functions. They involve enacting and enforcing the law, wielding public authority, and financing programs of prevention, deterrence, rehabilitation or incarceration.

As is readily apparent in the United States' defense industry, the modern view of government's exclusive powers in this domain allows for some complexity. The largest portion of dollars to produce the goods for our national defense is routed through the federal government to private contractors. It is Lockheed, Grumman, General Electric, et al. who produce the weapons and other hardware of

Harold W. Demone, Jr., PhD, is Professor of Social Work at Rutgers University, New Brunswick, where he served for a decade as Dean.

Margaret Gibelman, DSW, is Executive Vice President, Asthma and Allergy Foundation of America, Washington, DC.

defense. Many services are also purchased. Similarly, the goods and, increasingly, services needed to protect public safety from the threats of individuals — offenders of one type or another — are increasingly provided by the private sector under contract to government. More than half the police in the United States and Canada are employed by the private sector. In the U.S., private security employs an estimated 1.1 million people. Expenditures for private security products and services are estimated at $22 billion for 1980, compared to federal, state, and local law enforcement expenditures of $14 billion for 1979 (U.S. Department of Justice, October 1984).

The public role, then, becomes increasingly mixed. When contracting is used, the public role is that of planner, financier and monitor, though ultimate accountability cannot be contracted. The government could contract evaluation or auditing, for example, retaining the policy and interpretive judgements.

Levinson (1985) identifies several ways in which the private sector is involved in corrections: planning of facilities; financing of construction; building of correctional facilities; managing the correctional facility; service contracts; and community-based programs. Consultation is another traditional role and volunteers have long been active in corrections, assuming many different responsibilities. Robbins (1986) adds another form of private sector involvement: private industry within the prisons. Here, the goal is to assist prisoners to become or return to being productive members of society by having them produce a product or perform a service that can compete in the marketplace. In addition, the "employee-prisoners" may earn a decent wage and develop skills.

Although it is "prisons for profit" that has most caught public and media attention, primary concern in this article is with service contracting and the use of the private sector for rehabilitation programs carried out in the community.

MYTHS AND REALITIES

All too often when attention is directed to one target, the major action is occurring elsewhere. The several bibliographies on the privatization of corrections are heavily weighted to articles and reports on the for-profit operation of public correctional facilities. The majority of the references are to articles in the daily press which more likely demonstrate interest in the phenomenon than an accurate description of events. One firm about which much has been written is the Correctional Corporation of America which, as of this writing, has yet to secure a contract to operate an adult correctional facility for male felons (Prisons. Still public, 1988).

There is action in correctional contracting. The study conducted by the Camps (1986) for the National Institute of Corrections included responses from fifty-two agencies representing fifty-four jurisdictions. They found twenty-nine juvenile and thirty-seven adult agencies in thirty-nine states and the District of Columbia purchasing thirty-three types of services and/or programs from the private sector.

The management of prisons was not in the top ten most frequently used services/programs. Rather, it was the human services that constituted those most frequently purchased from private sources. Physicians, health, mental health, community treatment centers, education, drug treatment, college programs, staff training, vocational training and counseling ranked numbers one to eleven (Ibid.). (Construction placed number five.) A number of correctional agencies plan to expand their contractual provisions. Most highly rated for growth in the future are food services (18 percent) and the canteen and commissary (12 percent). Estimated for expansion at the 10-11 percent level are contracted vocational training, prison industries, work release, staff training, drug treatment, health services, and recreational therapy (Camp & Camp, 1986).

A 1984-85 study of contracting by the Lyndon Johnson School of Public Affairs focused on in-prison health services. All of the thirteen states studied reported some health services contracting, ranging from very little (Arizona and Oklahoma) to complete reliance on contracting from one large provider (Delaware and Alabama; Bakeman, Jennings & Smith, 1986).

Four major types of contracts were examined, consisting of those between correctional agencies and: (1) large private vendors, (2) local individuals; (3) local hospitals or universities, and (4) state level interagency contracting, e.g., the state health department.

Illinois has a mixed system, using three of the four alternatives cited above. The claim is that state control is maintained by this procedure.

Delaware has a much leaner procedure, but also has a much

smaller population than Illinois. Delaware contracts with a single provider responsible for the entire health system. The contract is the key element; it must be well written, free of ambiguities, possessed of a clear monitoring process, provide for positive and negative sanctions and clear-cut termination procedures. The state reports positive results, as does Alabama.

Georgia uses contracts for its four large facilities. These contractors help the correctional institutions cope with problems of staff recruitment and retention. For their smaller facilities, they are moving back to in-house service provision, claiming it is less expensive.

The thirteen states on which data were collected provided little information about quality or competence or adequacy of the contracted services (Ibid.). As noted later in this article, one advantage of contracting is that it has freed the agencies to evaluate programs in a manner which could not be applied to their own direct operation.

The trend is clearly toward more contracting for correctional services. New Jersey is an example. For the four year period (end of fiscal year 1984 to end of fiscal year 1987), the state Department of Corrections reported a steady growth in contracted half-way house services. There were five contracted half-way houses in 1984, seven in 1985 and 1986, and eight in 1987. The total daily census grew proportionately, from 89 to 135 to 143 to 226. In context, the total adult and juvenile residents in state and county facilities at the same time went from 11,874 (1984) to 16,063 (1987) (New Jersey Department of Corrections, 1988).

New Jersey's correctional agency also contracts elsewhere for services. A fifty bed unit is purchased from an acute care general hospital. Medical care provided in the institutions; psychological testing, urine testing, and data processing are among the other contracted services. New Jersey is likely average in its range of contracted activities among state correctional authorities. Highly selective and cautious, contracting is expanding.

CONTRACTING TO MEET MULTIPLE GOALS

As will be discussed below, the goal of the correctional system to deter and punish is also accompanied by the goal to rehabilitate. Thus, it is not surprising that the trend toward privatizing the field of corrections includes the human services elements in addition to the more concrete areas of construction, maintenance, and management.

There are three points in the correctional process in which the focus on the individual offender may be on rehabilitation; it is also at these points where the offender may come under the jurisdiction of the private sector (in addition to, or exclusive of privately managed prisons, per se): (1) when rehabilitation/treatment is seen as an alternative to incarceration; (2) while in prison to prepare the offender for the outside world and decrease repetitive criminal behavior, and (3) where treatment/rehabilitation is offered as a condition of release and/or parole.

In the latter instance, private sector services are purchased to provide offenders, who are eligible for release or who have been paroled into the community, the help they need for the transition and to reduce the likelihood they will return to criminal behavior in the future, and thus the jurisdiction of the correctional system. Examples include beds in privately managed half-way houses, job training programs, counseling, vocational counseling, and socialization skill training.

The goals attendant to the privatization of corrections, no matter whether the focus is on prevention, deterrence, incarceration, or post-incarceration rehabilitation, are similar: to save money, reduce capital expenditures, provide more effective and efficient services, and bypass the rigidity, slowness, and lack of responsiveness of public bureaucracies. None of this is new to government. Privatizing corrections has stimulated some additional questions, arising from the perceived purely public nature of the functions: to what extent can government delegate its authority in this area; to what extent can it hold the private sector accountable for the services/products delivered; can the interests and rights of the individuals be protected when accountability and authority are dispersed; and how can the goals of cost effectiveness and efficiency through use of the private sector be reconciled with the powers, duties, and responsibilities of government in relation to maintaining public safety, ensuring due process of law, etc.

There is also the inherent conflict between the public's clamor for safety and protection against offenders and the concept and practice of rehabilitation. "Dumping" of offenders from prisons to the community, where rehabilitation would be administered under the nominal authority of the parole board, would ordinarily not be the safety valve for the prison system, as it is for mental hospitals or institutions for the retarded. However, in light of the severe overcrowding of prisons and court intervention to ensure at least minimal prison standards, such "dumping" into the community is actually occurring, particularly in large metropolitan areas such as the District of Columbia and New York City (Hockstader, June 9, 1988). The pressures remain on the prisons, but the urgency of overcrowding and the edict to do something about it has diminished the countervailing community influence. Thus, the use of community "services," whether in a custodial or rehabilitative mode, is now more than ever an issue. It is also a rare opportunity for those who are committed to alternatives to imprisonment.

REHABILITATION AND THE PRIVATE SECTOR

The use of the private (not-for-profit) sector to provide correctional services (within or outside of the institutional setting), particularly those focused on rehabilitation, was given great impetus in the 1960s, in conjunction with the general expansion of human services programs under "The Great Society." The "culture of poverty" concept, combined with views about the poor, delinquent, and even criminal as "victims" of social forces ("blaming the victim"), translated into service programs to provide the educational, vocational and life skills to compensate for and overcome past individual deficiencies. Other relevant philosophical underpinnings of the rehabilitation movement, also products of the 1960s "liberalism," were the belief in the sanctity of the individual, the absolute priority afforded the needs of minorities and the poor, and a distrust of institutional means of dealing with social issues. The attitude that society was at least partially responsible for deviant behavior and that criminal behavior was a manifestation of social conditions and forces over which an individual might not have control, was also a major force in molding adaptation-oriented programs. Decriminalization of public intoxication led to a rapid decline in the censuses of institutions for misdeamenants. State institutions, including prisons, became likely targets of the reform movement, since they were overwhelmingly and disproportionately populated by minorities and the poor (Miller, 1977). Offenders were, therefore, to be rehabilitated, rather than punished, along with similar attempts in regard to the mentally ill, delinquent, and retarded. These adaptational, individually oriented processes were to occur outside of prisons or jails, reflecting the early stages of the deinstitutionalization movement.

Equally as important as the philosophical and value based stance toward those outside the mainstream of society was the availability of government funds to initiate rehabilitation programs. (One can always question whether philosophy follows the dollars, or whether it is the prevalent philosophy that dictates where the dollars go.)

MENTAL HEALTH

It was the community mental health movement, one of the benefactees of the War on Poverty and Great Society programs, that was delegated a significant role in providing the rehabilitation services for offenders, past, current, or potential. According to Krajick (1984), it was nonprofit (and a few for-profit) agencies, such as community mental health centers, that supplied many of the most progressive community programs for offenders, including halfway houses, work programs, and drug rehabilitation programs, under purchase of service arrangements with government agencies.

The use of community mental health centers to provide rehabilitation services under purchase of service contract was a logical step. The anti-bureaucracy, anti-government (as service provider) sentiments were accompanied by a pro-community, pro-grass roots services preference, including an emphasis on self-help.

Despite the media attention devoted to for-profits, the major actors are to be found in the public and not-for-profit sectors, with the latter demonstrating the larger absolute growth. In 1987, agency auspice was as follows: not-for-profit, 78 percent; public, 21 percent; and for-profit, 1 percent (National Council of Community Mental Health Centers, 1987). These partnerships are well embedded and long-standing in the entire social welfare arena, with adult and juvenile criminal justice, alcohol and drug abuse and mental health consistently showing the larger shifts from public to voluntary auspices. In 1986, for example, 1.9 percent of reporting community mental health agencies (under voluntary auspices) provided specific forensic programs for special populations; in 1987, this percentage had risen to 16. Fifty-five percent of the agencies offered special programs for substance abusers (ibid.).

That the rehabilitation was to occur outside of the institutional setting (in the form of prevention, alternatives to incarceration, or early offender release) had much to do with the courts, which themselves became centers of change with a focus on procedural protections, including the right to a lawyer, due process and parole review. A major factor affecting the involvement of the courts in dispensing "rehabilitation justice" was the result of a 1966 decision by Judge David Bazelon, who articulated a "constitutional right to treatment," which had been advanced by Dr. Morton Birnbaum several years earlier (Miller, 1977). In the years following Judge Bazelon's decision in *Rouse v. Cameron*, "the right to treatment" has provided the legal basis for many actions against public institutions by civil liberty groups, child advocacy groups, and the Department of Justice.

The courts' interpretation of the "right to treatment" had its constitutional foundations in early habeas corpus actions on behalf of citizens held in correctional institutions for non-penal reasons. Miller attributes the expansion of such court actions as the basis for rulings that confinement must be in a place where conditions are actually therapeutic, challenging confinement on the grounds that no treatment is given. A premise is that it is society's obligation to provide treatment and/or rehabilitation in exchange for the denial of the liberty to the mentally ill or criminal (Miller, p. 97).

PROS AND CONS OF PRIVATIZATION

Those who hold a "minimalist" view of government's functions would naturally be inclined to see any privatization as positive. Others are more selective in their evaluation. Lerman, in his comprehensive review of the juvenile justice system, writes of the "private entrepreneurial types" who deal effectively in our free market heritage (1982, p. 33). In his view, they can provide new services and offer new programs, be they of a profit or not-for-profit nature.

Lerman sees society as supportive of those who can perform a personal service and achieve personal gain.

Although public sentiment favors "stiffer" penalties for offenders, including longer periods of incarceration, policy makers must weigh the goals of deterrence and punishment against the legal and practical considerations concerning the current state of America's prisons and jails. According to Robbins (1986), more than two-thirds of the states are under court order to correct conditions that violate constitutional prohibitions against cruel and unusual punishment. Within the category of "cruel and unusual punishment" is the overcrowded state of prisons and jails. The cost of incarceration (up to $60 per day per inmate) is also leading policy makers and corrections experts to look for alternatives.

Given the current emphasis on privatization, it is not surprising that some in the corrections field have adopted this concept as their own. They believe that removing the operations, and sometimes ownership, of prisons and jails from local, state, or federal governments and turning these functions over to private corporations will increase efficiency and ultimately reduce costs.

As noted earlier, there are limits established by the federal Constitution, as well as other institutional restrictions. Kuttner (1987) observes several institutional settings in which private market forces are inappropriate. Such areas include the psychological, religious, familial, health and social, where "cost savings" or "efficiency" or "free enterprise" as the operating principles are simply beside the point; civic, public values and goals are very much the point. Given the social purposes of some government functions and programs, contracting also poses some serious accountability issues to ensure equity, equality, fair distribution, etc. According to Kuttner (1987, p. 7):

> . . . the appeals of contracting-out government become less apparent when one takes a closer look. In theory, contracting-out government services brings to the public realm all the virtues of the private market—flexibility, innovation, and competition. In practice, however, contracting-out government begs the ancient political question: Quis custodiet ipsos custodes? (Who will watch the watchers?)

Miller, for one, believes that the community mental health centers' movement "failed to deliver on its vastly inflated promises" (1977, p. 96). Rather than discount the worth of privatization, one likely option was to decrease reliance on the non-profit sector in favor of the for-profit sector. The incentive of profit making, some believe, would entice these private contractors to deliver efficient and effective services, with efficiency measured in cost savings.

The use of the term "privatization" as descriptive of the use of the private sector to deliver some select criminal justice functions may be a misnomer. Privatization, in its sure sense, refers to the assumption of responsibility of non-public sources for functions heretofore within the public domain. When a service, product, or function is transferred to the private sector but fiscal and legal accountability still reside within the public sector, what we have, in essence, is the creation of quasi-public or quasi-private entities, depending on the degree of public dominance. One distinctive character of the ideal-type private sector organization, its independence of government control or financing, simply does not and cannot apply. It is thus unlikely that rehabilitation or any other criminal justice programs can be truly private. Instead, some of the characteristics of the private sector, such as governance by a board of directors (frequently composed, at least during the 1960s and early 1970s of community representatives and service consumers) and separate administrative structures, were replicated in not-for-profit agencies, but financing was predominantly or sometimes exclusively public. Some of these not-for-profits came into being precisely because of the availability of government funds and the government-directed new emphasis on de-institutional services (Smith, forthcoming).

To a substantial extent, the significant increase in private participation in correctional services is a function of the growth in available community alternatives. The demand created the market, eventually including some for-profits in addition to the voluntary agencies. Community mental health and alcohol treatment agencies, as two examples, looked to new and expanding sources of public and private (e.g., third party insurance) funds as the War on Poverty and public mental health dollars dried up. The timing was auspicious.

A key factor, of course, in whether the private sector is able to deliver the low cost, high quality, efficient rehabilitation services expected of it. One obvious problem with preventive or post-incarceration rehabilitation is that "success" may well depend on the ability to manipulate the larger environment in which the offender functions. A good proportion of offenders are not "sick" in the clinical sense (with, perhaps, the exception of the violent person) but rather the product of several interacting forces, including psychological, environmental and social. (It should be recalled that one important premise for reinvigorating the rehabilitation approach was the "culture of poverty" philosophy.)

Recently, social scientists have alluded to the "worsening plight of the underclass" as a variable in the growing crime rate. Coughlin (1988, p. A5) enunciates what the newspapers tell us every day: the ghetto poor are afflicted with "social pathologies," including drug abuse, chronic unemployment, welfare dependency and crime. Taken together or separately, these afflictions appear to be "impervious to change."

The lack of upward mobility, or in the terminology of the 1960s, "opportunity," suggests that the released offender is likely to return to the same or similar environment that promoted or encouraged the criminal behavior in the first instance. And although community or other private agencies may attempt to focus on the "person within their environment," options for manipulating that environment have decreased significantly with the federal cutbacks in almost all social services, public health, and job training programs.

ACCOUNTABILITY

As discussed above, the treatment of offenders can never be an exclusively private enterprise, but rather a sharing of public and private functions. The offender is, in most cases, an involuntary participant in treatment. As such, it is the power of the courts and/or correctional system that provides the incentive to force the offender into treatment. The private sector may act on behalf of the criminal justice system, but lacks the authority to completely replace it or to mandate participation. The fact that the private sector may provide an administrative, psychological, medical or social service role under contract does not render the public sector void of responsibility. It is only the public sector, with its constitutional authority and legal responsibility for public safety and law and order, that can wield such coercive powers.

The exclusive powers and responsibilities of government within the domain of criminal justice has been established in a number of court cases that have focused on the questions of liability when these public functions are contracted to the private sector. Several decisions placing responsibility and accountability squarely on the shoulders of government have been based on the Federal Civil Rights Act, 42 U.S.C. 1983, which has been interpreted to mean that government liability in lawsuits that may be brought by inmates or prison employees cannot be shifted and that government does not have the power to delegate authority for criminal justice (Robbins, 1986). The problem, notes Robbins, is fundamental to two constitutional rights, the Fifth and Fourteenth amendments, which prohibit the government from denying federal constitutional rights and which guarantee due process of law. These Amendments apply to the acts of the state and federal governments, not to the acts of private parties or entities, even if the latter are acting on behalf of government. The liability of the state remains intact, particularly given the involuntary nature of confinement, the detailed nature of the contracts between the government and the private entities, the level of government funding, and the extent of state regulation of policies and programs.

Although some states have argued that they are not liable for the acts of a private corporation, such as in a suit (*Lombard v. Eunice Kennedy Shriver Center* (556 F. Supp. 677, D. Mass. 1983), where it was alleged that a resident of a state institution was denied adequate medical care, the courts have ruled that the "critical factor in our decision is the duty of the state to provide adequate medical services to those whose personal freedom is restricted because they reside in state institutions." Further, the court ruled that:

> Because the state bore an affirmative obligation to provide adequate medical care to plaintiff, because the state delegated that function to the (private corporation), and because (that corporation) voluntarily assumed that obligation by contract,

(the private entity) must be considered to have acted under color of law, and its acts and omissions must be considered actions of the state. For if (the private entity) were not held so responsible, the state could avoid its constitutional obligations simply by delegating governmental functions to private entities. (as quoted in Robbins, 1986, p. 329)

Robbins notes that the courts have been consistent in their rulings, and that the state has been deemed responsible and liable when any form of detention is in question, including involuntary participation in a mental health center program.

The weight of opinion is that privatization of corrections cannot include the dispensing of ultimate accountability. Nor can privatization be complete in the sense of financial independence from the public sector. Prisons may be able to be run on a profit basis (most of the evidence, however, is still pending on this), but services—medical, psychological, social and educational are seldom, if ever, subject to the same kinds of market generating forces. Some may be self-supporting. About half of the nation's health care expenditures come from third party fees. But who is to pay for the rehabilitation of ex-offenders? Since the individuals are referred, often involuntarily, by the corrections system for services and may still be under the jurisdiction of that system, it is the public agency that logically maintains financial responsibility. This is totally consistent with the public interest. The most common model is that of purchase of service, wherein the correctional system provides the funds, under grant or contract, for non-profit or for-profit community agencies to deliver the rehabilitation/treatment services. Whether purchasing costs the government more or less than direct provision, the full burden of payment still resides with the public agency.

The delegation of service provision to the private sector may, in fact, facilitate the public agency's role of monitoring and ensuring accountability. Partnerships with the private sector eliminate the problem of internal monitoring. Monitoring of externally delivered programs reduces the conflict of interest found in vertical organizations and allows for more efficient role delegation. Regulation and the provision of technical assistance become logical extensions of the public sector role.

Assuring accountability through the regulatory role is, however, a complicated business, particularly in the field of corrections. The regulatory industry lacks consistency (Lourie, 1979). The health arena is characterized by professional licensure, standards, accreditation, and peer review. The criminal justice system, including corrections and juvenile justice, has extremely limited external controls. Rehabilitation is equally uncontrolled, except for the recent development of an accreditation program for sheltered workshops. Similarly, there is a lack of widespread external certification and licensure for the professionals practicing within the vocational rehabilitation field. (Of course, the rehabilitation counselor acts as a case manager, a potentially powerful monitoring tool.) Psychologists, physicians and nurses are licensed in all states, social workers in most, and family therapists in the majority. The variability of standards must surely impact on the ability of the public agency to maintain its regulatory role.

EVALUATION

Any assessment of the value (measured in qualitative, quantitative, comparative — public vs. private — and outcome terms) of privately offered rehabilitation services must address two somewhat distinct issues: (1) the value of the rehabilitation approach, per se, which may or may not have anything to do with the auspices under which such services are delivered, and (2) the effectiveness of the private sector in delivering rehabilitation services.

As contracting for rehabilitation services has expanded, so have evaluation/recidivism studies. The same occurrence has been observed in relation to public social service and community mental health agencies. This phenomenon is neither unexpected nor counterproductive. It is always easier to evaluate the works of others than that of colleagues, especially if the judgment might be less than favorable.

Given the relatively recent status of contracting for offender rehabilitation services and the general lack of hard evaluative data on privatization across all fields, it is not surprising that the literature is predominantly descriptive or theoretical rather than empirically based. One evaluation study of note was that conducted to determine the outcome of a contracted program to run a juvenile correction facility (Levinson, 1985). In 1982, the State of Florida transferred the Okeechobee School for Boys (a 400 bed, secure facility for adjudicated delinquents) from the Department of Health and Rehabilitative Services to a private, not-for-profit agency. The contract was predicated on the belief (by the state agency) that the transfer would result in cost savings while concurrently delivering a program of equal or better quality. The conduct of an independent evaluation was built into the contract.

The evaluation effort was thwarted by a number of methodological and practical problems, including the difficulty in locating a suitable control group, incomplete information, and lack of comparable data. Based on the data collected, the contracted program appeared to be equal in quality to that conducted by the state. There were no significant reductions in operational costs. Overall, the results did not reveal strong support for the use of private agencies as an alternative management strategy (Levinson, 1985).

That evaluation studies often conclude that the measured interventions were of limited value and sometimes without effect is also not surprising. The same was true of nearly all of the early Head Start follow-up studies. Not until fifteen to twenty years had ensued were the differences clear and positive. It may well be that there are two major errors in the research strategy: overdependence on single outcome measures (e.g., school grades or recidivism) and a much too brief time frame.

Although monitoring and evaluation have similar superordinate objectives and inhabit the same continuum, they are substantially unlike in their process. Evaluation is in the research mainstream. Methodological canons must be observed. Monitoring can be accomplished in several ways, although product appraisal is clearly the best choice. Failing that, we opt for ensuring the competence of the agents hired by the provider. The third best monitoring tool may focus on the quality and frequency of the supervision.

At the low end of monitoring efficiency and effectiveness is the request for and delivery of process reports. They reduce the service effort and are largely unread. Reports are necessary, but they deserve careful design attention.

The "social value" benefits of rehabilitation may have merit beyond the impact on particular individuals. One social value benefit may lie in the fact that rehabilitation offers the public tangible evidence that "something" is being done to deter criminal behavior, even if that "something" has not yet shown the expected results. The weight of public opinion, judges, and correctional officers, also may favor a "helping" strategy, particularly after incarceration. A prison term signifies society's punishment. Given the historic ambivalence about the causation of criminal behavior ("bad person" versus "bad environment inducing bad behavior"), this society may well need to blend punishment with rehabilitative efforts.

The ability of the private sector to deliver rehabilitation services in the best interests of the offender may be marred by the profit motive. According to Robbins (1986, p. 326) "the private sector is more interested in doing well than in doing good"; humanitarian values are secondary, if at all existent, to the profit-making goal.

Evaluating the use of private sector services from a cost perspective, one former juvenile corrections commissioner stated that "Private enterprise probably *can* run prisons cheaper than government. The question is, are they just going to run an outmoded and inhumane system more efficiently, or are they going to bring some real improvements and new ideas?" (J. Miller, as quoted in Krajick, 1984, p. 9).

It is, however, important to reiterate that the private sector is composed of two different forms: not-for-profit and for-profit. Although it is the profit sector that has significantly entered the ownership, management, and product servicing of jails and prisons, most of the "softer," labor intensive areas within the correction field, such as mental and physical health care and vocational rehabilitation, fall to the not-for-profit sector. Here, the profit motive is secondary to the humanitarian motive. Although not-for-profits need to ensure that their operating costs are met and some is left over for "overhead" (administrative costs), which are often solicited and negotiated as part of the contract, "making a buck" is not what it is all about.

CAUTIONS

If the privatization experiences of other fields, ranging from defense to social services, are referenced to guide the present and future (as they should be), there are some essential cautions that must be observed by both government and the private sector in applying contracting theories and practice to corrections.

Government

1. Although the governmental agency will need fewer employees, given privatization, they will need to be better trained and more experienced. They must have the skills in the substantive area covered by the contract, be possessed of professional competence, and have managerial capacity.

2. It must be clear about its objectives.

3. It should focus on outcome measures.

4. It should try to establish some experimental situations, such as contracting in one setting and directly managing and operating in another. With competent assistance secured, government should then compare the results.

5. The more professional the service, the more likely it should be contracted. High standards for personnel should be established.

6. Efforts should be made to collaborate with colleges and universities, starting with the state land grant university which has over 100 years of experience in working with state and federal agencies.

Providers

1. Providers should avoid bidding on or competing for contracts outside of their area of competence.

2. They should resist or reject contract provisions that apply governmental personnel procedures to provider agencies. Such provisions tend to be anachronistic, formalistic, and cost intensive.

3. They should resist strongly the exercise of line item budget practices and control. The continuation of governmental personnel and fiscal practices (and, to some degree, purchasing), all designed for zero error objectives, have created highly inefficient organiza-

tions. These procedures should not be forced upon the provider agencies. Salary structures of voluntary agencies, for example, are internal matters and not the business of government.

EXPANDING CORRECTIONAL TREATMENT SERVICES THROUGH CONTRACTING

Given the extent of current service contracting (76 percent for physicians to 39 percent for counseling), the continued expansion of private sector resources within corrections has obvious limits. Of the ten most frequently purchased services (exclusive of construction), five are already at the 50 percent level. Even if all ten of the services were fully contracted, it would bring the total national expenditures for private sector services to about $400 million or 12 percent of the budget. The budgets of institutionally based agencies are highly fixed; the variable ratio very small.

Significant growth can occur only by absolute service expansion, as has been the case in the fields of alcoholism and drug abuse. Such expansion for rehabilitation/treatment services for offenders would necessarily involve some ideological, legal and regulatory shifts within the corrections system. (Impetus for such shifts may, however, come about with continued pressure to address overcrowded prison conditions, a practical rather than philosophical matter.) The other alternative is, of course, to contract the entire institution.

CONCLUSION

What seems to be actually happening in corrections, in contrast to the doomsayers, is consistent with the new reform liberalism. In this view, government is not the enemy (as Presidents Carter and Reagan believed in rationalizing the focus on privatization), nor is government seen as the ultimate ideal force to support and service all human needs. Rather, government, with its eye on equity and concern for all of its citizens, should be prepared to lead or follow, as may be required. Cooperation and collaboration across boundaries and sectors is legitimate, one form of which is the purchase of services from the private sector.

Although there are some special features to the public-private partnership in the field of corrections, each new collaboration brings its own set of circumstances and constraints. To varying degrees, all partnerships involve ultimate accountability by government, monitoring of the use of public funds, assurances of equity, and, in the case of corrections, responsibility for ensuring public safety. With clarity about these governmental mandates, there is still an enormous role that can be assumed by the private sector.

REFERENCES

Bakeman, B. A., Jennings, B. & Smith, L. (1986). Contracting for medical services in selected Texas state institutions and agencies, pp. 93-136. In Blodgett, T. and Chapman, J. (1986). *Contracting selected state government functions: Issues and next steps* (Policy Research Project Report No. 75). Austin, TX: Lyndon B. Johnson School of Public Affairs, The University of Texas.

Camp, C. & Camp, G. (1985, Autumn/Winter). Correctional privatization in perspective. *The Prison Journal*, 14-31.

Coughlin, Ellen K. (1988, March 30). Worsening plight of the 'underclass' catches attention of researchers. *The Chronicle of Higher Education*, pp. A5, A7.

Hockstader, L. (9 June 1988). "D.C. urged to move or free inmates." *Washington Post*, D5.

Krajick, K. (1984, April). Prisons for profit: The private alternative. *State Legislatures, 10*, 9-14.

Kuttner, R. (1987, Spring). Viewpoint: The private market can't always solve public problems, *The Privatization Review, 2*(2), 6-7.

Lerman, P. (1982). *Deistitutionalization and the welfare state*. New Brunswick, NJ: Rutgers University Press.

Levinson, R. B. (1985, Autumn/Winter). Okeechobee: An evaluation of privatization in corrections. *The Prison Journal*, 75-94.

Lourie, N. (1979). Purchase of service contracting: Issues confronting the government sponsored agency, pp. 18-29. In Wedel, K. R., Katz, A. J. and Weick, A. (eds.), *Social services by government contract: A policy analysis*. NY: Praeger.

Miller, H. L. (1977, Winter). The 'right to treatment': Can the courts rehabilitate and cure? *The Public Interest, 46*, 96-118.

National Council of Community Mental Health Centers (1985, April). *Membership profile report*. Rockville, MD.

New Jersey Department of Corrections (1988, January). Admissions, releases and residents. Trenton, NJ.

Prisons. Still public. (1988, February 27). *The Economist*, p. 47.

Robbins, I. P. (1986, April/May). Privatization of corrections: Defining the issues. *Judicature, 69*, 324-221.

Smith, S. R. (1989, forthcoming). Federal funding, nonprofit agencies, and victim services. In Demone, H.W. and Gibelman, M. (eds.) *Services for Sale: Purchasing Health and Human Services*. New Brunswick, NJ: Rutgers University Press.

United States Department of Justice, National Institute of Justice. (1984, October). *The growing role of private security* (Research in Brief).

Wilson, J. Q. and Boland, B. (1976). Crime, pp. 179-230. In Gorham, W. and Glazer, N. (eds.). *The Urban Predicament*. Washington, DC: The Urban Institute.

Men Who Abuse Their Spouses: Social and Psychological Supports

Jessica R. Davidovich

SUMMARY. This paper explores psychological variables which have been identified as characteristic of males who physically abuse their partners in an attempt to determine which psychological variables explain the acts of the violently abusive male who engages in spouse abuse.

LEGITIMIZATION OF WIFE ABUSE

Wife abuse has been studied from a number of perspectives. Undoubtedly, the area of the role of social and legal forces is, and has been, the most widely studied to date.

Wife abuse, although a serious social problem in many societies, has not always been viewed as a crime. Wife-beating was permitted by law in the United States until the late 19th century. Common law provided that men could beat their wives with a switch as long as the switch was not wider than the width of their thumbs (Roy, 1982). Social change, however, has brought with it an atmosphere conducive to legal changes. In the United States it is only recently that the courts have recognized wife abuse as a crime. Consequently, wife abusers are only now beginning to be held reprehensible for their actions under the eyes of the law. The shroud of family secrecy is no longer more important than the individual welfare of family members. Changes in norms and value systems have brought

Jessica R. Davidovich teaches undergraduate courses in sociology and criminal justice at the College of Arts & Sciences on the Newark Campus of Rutgers University, where she is pursuing a doctorate in the Graduate School of Criminal Justice.

27

forth important changes in laws as well as public awareness and sensitivity to the problems of family violence.

Social and legal change concerning wife abuse has taken place in other cultures as well. For example, this passage from the Holy Qur'an is a powerful illustration of the phenomenon of wife-beating in Islamic cultures.

> Men are the protectors
> And maintainers of women,
> Because God has given
> The one more (strength)
> Than the other, and because
> They support them
> From their means.
> Therefore the righteous women
> Are devoutly obedient, and guard
> In (the husband's) absence,
> What God would have them guard.
>
> As to those women
> On whose part ye fear
> Disloyalty and ill-conduct,
> Admonish them (first),
> (Next) refuse to share their beds,
> (And last) beat them (lightly).
> But if they return to obedience,
> Seek not against them
> Means (of annoyance).
>
> *— The Holy Qur'an*, p.190

The Holy Qur'an, ancient though it may be, lays out a few significant social dimensions of wife abuse that have been recognized by social scientists as conditions which promote and perpetuate violence against wives in their homes. Because religion and law are one in Islamic cultures, it is not only a privilege of a husband to beat his wife, but it is accorded to him as a duty to do so when his wife disobeys him. Secondly, this right of a man to beat his wife is grounded in the historical economic dependence of woman upon man for means of support. Mention is also made of a woman's natural duty to remain chaste and pure. Although taken from Islamic culture, these ideas, which have perpetuated violence against women in many of the Middle Eastern countries, have historically been present in Western society as well.

Socialization and enculturation are central to the shaping and limiting of male and female boundaries and social roles in every culture. As the social roles were embedded in the societal structure, *haves* and *have-nots* resulted under patriarchal family systems (Dobash and Dobash, 1979). The men historically have had the power, and women and children were subject to the authority of the head of the household (Jennings, 1987). Indeed much of the sociological literature of wife abuse has documented the results of male domination in the patriarchal family system.

Research has also pinpointed the strongest variable in a woman's decision to remain in a physically abusive situation (Kalmuss and Straus, 1982). Economic factors tended to be the strongest reasons why women continue to remain in households where they are physically abused. Generally, researchers have generated a wealth of knowledge about *victims* of wife abuse.

Even in the most conservative society in the world (see Adler, 1983), social change has brought forth changes in Saudi Arabian law on wife abuse. Modern law attempts to concur with the Holy Qur'an, but places limitations on the amount of corporal punishment a husband may inflict upon his wife. The law clearly states that only certain areas of the woman's body may be beaten by her husband (Audah, 1983). Specifically, the area between the neck and thighs is not permitted to be subject to any type of battery (Audah, 1983). Secondly, the law states that a husband may not inflict injury which results in broken bones, contusions or marks on the woman's body (Audah, 1983). Any woman in Saudi Arabia who sustains serious bodily injury resulting from wife abuse is permitted to seek legal redress in order to prevent further harm to herself.

There is little doubt that social and legal forces are part and parcel of the problem of wife abuse. The same factors which permit wife abuse are also responsible for legitimizing other types of family violence, such as elder abuse (referred to as *granny-bashing* and *gram-slamming* in the sociological literature) as well as child abuse.

Further, sociocultural causes of family violence are a valuable source of information about the dynamics of family violence.

Cross-cultural comparisons elucidate the impact of loosening external controls on the family. Familial controls, residential mobility, weakening of parental authority and the generally increasing state of anomie have contributed to higher rates of family violence, particularly in American society (Levine, 1985; Witt, 1987).

There has been, however, a disturbingly small amount of research done about the *batterers* themselves. Part of the reason may be the slow change from the historical acceptance of wife abuse to the perspective that wife abuse is a crime and should be treated as such. Consequently, convenient samples just did not exist for the purposes of study.

Today, however, as spouse abusers are arrested more frequently and mandated by courts to undergo treatment programs (Ganley, 1981; Goolkasian, 1986), a "convenient" population sample of males engaging in spouse abuse is beginning to form. Indeed, it has only been within the past seven years that the criminal justice system has begun to play a more active role in prosecuting spouse abusers (Goolkasian, 1986; Soler, 1987). It is time for researchers to begin extensive systematic study of the battering population themselves, as well as of situational variables associated with spouse abuse. Yet, we know too little about batterers to determine which treatment programs and formats are most effective in helping batterers desist from violent behaviors. Few direct studies of batterers have been done to date using reliable psychological measures (Jennings, 1987). Recent research on psychological variables of males engaging in spouse abuse is the beginning of an understanding of the batterer. Understanding psychological variables is necessary to refine, supplement and extend what is currently known about wife abuse (Hamberger and Hastings, 1988).

THE PSYCHOLOGY OF BATTERING

Psychological theories focusing on wife abuse fall into one of three categories: (a) personality explanations, (b) the social learning theory and (c) the psychodynamic explanations.

The Personality Perspective

Hamberger and Hastings (1986) suggest that (1) psycopathology is higher in batterers than non-batterers and (2) "spouse abusers exhibit personality characteristics which predispose them to difficulties in coping with stress in intimate relationships." It is from this perspective that researchers studying the psychological variables associated with males engaging in spouse abuse have attempted to develop a more comprehensive view of the batterer in his social context (Kihlstrom, 1987).

The first and foremost attempt to understand the psychology of batterers was presented by Elbow (1977). Although no systematic statistical analysis was utilized, the study provided descriptive data about four patterns of behavior identified in batterers. Elbow (1977) begins with the theoretical assumption that marriage is an attempt to maintain a state of homeostasis in an individual's life. It is when coping mechanisms fail, and the batterer's ego is ruptured, that males then resort to violence in intimate relationships.

Elbow (1977) further identified four personality characteristics of batterers. These are:

1. The batterer transfers blame for marital conflict onto his partner and denies responsibility.
2. The batterer is threatened by his wife's autonomy. He is also overly dependent upon his wife to fulfill all his emotional needs. Therefore, he isolates himself from friends and expects his wife to do the same.
3. There is a strong tendency for the batterer to "parentify" his wife, viewing her much in the same way he perceives his mother. Thus, he repeats conflicts/emotional struggles that he had with his mother as a child.
4. He has rigid expectations of his wife, and expects her to conform to them at all times.

Basically, Elbow (1977) felt that four types of abuse syndromes develop in batterers. Each syndrome centers on a different emotional need experienced by the batterer. The batterer attempts to fulfill this need through his wife.

Elbow's formulation has had a profound influence on the types of treatment programs implemented for men who batter. There is a general belief that batterers are by and large an isolated group who are extremely dependent upon their wives to fulfill emotional needs (Roy, 1982; Jennings, 1987). Support consistent with these findings has come from both clinical and observational reports, as well as from empirical studies.

Hofeller (1983) regards the batterer as having the following personality characteristics:

- Insecurity
- Poor Verbal Communication
- Dominating
- Dual Personality — (Dr. Jekyll/Hyde)
- Lack of Assertiveness

Hofeller's (1983) report lacks an empirical basis. Observational reports providing descriptive and demographic data about the batterers are not included. As such, there is no way to conclude that these characteristics are not common to all men. It may indeed be that traditional sex-role expectations are so pervasive that it is not possible to differentiate between violent and nonviolent men by merely using intuitive beliefs as parameters on the personality characteristics of batterers.

There is recent scientific evidence that batterers exhibit disorder in basic personality processes (Hamberger and Hastings, 1986). Using a sample of 105 batterers from a court-mandated treatment program, Hamberger and Hastings (1986) employed the Millon Clinical Multiaxial Inventory (MCMI) to examine personality profiles of batterers. Considerable dysphoria (depression and anger proneness) was noted among the pathological profiles. Three major personality factors were revealed among batterers:

1. Schizoid/Borderline
2. Narcissistic/Antisocial
3. Passive dependent/Compulsive

Hamberger and Hastings (1986) conducted an exploratory study which did not utilize control groups. The findings of a follow-up study replicated the results of the original exploratory study, with factor analysis used to confirm the three categories of personalities. Thus, the authors concluded that maladaptive personality character- istics contribute to spouse abuse. Dysphoria was also found to a large extent in the sample of batterers used in the second study.

Hamberger and Hastings (1988) validated their previous two studies with yet another study which was successful in both validat- ing their original results and clarifying their findings. Using the Millon Clinical Multiaxial Inventory (MCMI), the NOVACO An- ger Scale and the Beck Depression Inventory, Hamberger and Hast- ings (1988) studied a sample of 43 males (22 of whom reported marital discordance and 21 marital satisfaction). Among their find- ings was that alcoholic abusive batterers tended to be classified as Schizoid/Borderline personalities. Non-batterers tended to score higher on the Dependency/Compulsivity factors.

Hamberger and Hastings (1988) interpreted these findings to sug- gest that batterers show a higher degree of histrionicity. That is, they deliberately display emotions on the basis of the perceived social effect it will incur. This may explain the Dr. Jekyll/Mr. Hyde personality observed by numerous clinicians (Elbow, 1977). Ham- berger and Hastings (1988) characterize the batterers as demonstrat- ing initially charming and socially appropriate behaviors. However, when the batterer's sense of control is threatened, negative features inherent in his personality emerge, through demonstrations of vio- lence and intimidation directed at his target(s). Further, Hamberger and Hastings (1988) hold that batterers generally have a distorted view of reality, leaning toward psychotic interpretations of events and situations. This interpretation provides the basis for understand- ing the alternating behavioral pattern seen in the individual batterer, which vacillates from calm and prosocial behavior to sullen, vindic- tive and abusive behavior.

Empirical research documenting the high rates of dysphoria (an- ger-proneness) and depression in the battering population has been supported in a number of studies.

Maiuro, Cahn and their associates (1988) sampled 129 males, arrayed into four comparison groups: domestically violent men, two groups of generally assaultive men (non-family violence only) and a non-violent control group. On the basis of the Buss-Durkee Hostil- ity Inventory, the Hostility and Direction of Hostility Questionnaire and the Beck Depression Inventory, Maiuro and Cahn (1988) concluded that domestically violent men were more likely to be depressed than were the comparison groups. Additionally, scores reflecting anger and hostility were similar for both the domestically violent men and the generally assaultive male category. These findings imply that batterers can generally be characterized as a depressed group. Further, violent behavior may be linked to the amount of anger and hostility in an individual in general, regardless of the type of violent behavior. Consequently, Maiuro and Cahn (1988) postulate that circumscribed psychological problems potentiate violent outbursts, at least among the males from the lower socioeconomic strata who comprised their sample.

Shuerger and Reigle (1988) attempted to examine more closely schizoid disorder in males engaging in spouse abuse. They studied 32 males from a group of 250 who had participated in a court-ordered treatment program. The Michigan Alcohol Screening Test, the Violence Inventory (adapted from Straus's Conflict Tactics Scales), the IDEA Inventory (a test of irrational thoughts and behavior), and the Psychological Screening Inventory were administered. Shuerger and Reigle (1988) found that batterers exhibited high rates of psychopathology, including anxiety, depression and schizoid tendencies, thus consistent with the findings of previous research (Elbow, 1977; Hamberger and Hastings, 1988; Maiuro and Cahn, 1988).

Personality and the Power Variable

Personality and attitudinal characteristics have been examined from a sex-role identity perspective. Rosenbaum (1986) concluded that batterers tended to be less masculine, less feminine and more likely "undifferentiated" as a group. The underlying rationale is that males who are undifferentiated lack sex-role identity and thus adopt a behavioral pattern on the basis of their perception of what a man should be or represent. Violence is the result of an individual's embracing the conception of maleness which stems from the macho male image promoted in society.

Another avenue of the personality and power assessment explored by researchers is the male motivational need for power. A study by Dutton and Strachan (1987) measured males attitudes toward women, the need for power and the level of assertiveness in males who engage in spouse abuse. The sample included 25 domestically violent men, 25 maritally conflicted nonassaultive males and 25 demographically matched males who reported no violence with harmonious marital relationships. The measurement instruments used in this study were the Thematic Apperception Test and the Spouse Specific Assertiveness Scales. Discriminant analysis revealed that the need for power, as well as a lack of verbal skills, correctly classified wife assaulters 90 percent of the time (Dutton and Strachan, 1987). They interpret their findings as indicating domestically assaultive men have a high need for power, yet lack verbal resources to control power in an intimate relationship. Thereby, chronic frustration is produced in the batterer, and, thus, there is an increased likelihood that he will resort to the use of violence. Violence and aggression serve a communicational function, conveying the batterers' desire to control power.

Another issue is that violence then appears to be motivated as well as deliberate, i.e., directed to achieving some goal, whether it is conscious or subconscious. Thus, the findings of Dutton and Strachan (1987) are consistent with those of Hamberger and Hastings (1988), who had concluded that batterers are highly histrionic. That is, batterers deliberately display emotions on the basis of the perceived social effect it will incur. This element is also recognized, although not explicitly, by Toch (1986), who suggests that women in spousal abuse situations are a defenseless optimal audience for the abuser's actions, with the short-term motive of immediately relieving chronic frustration and the long-term motives of maintaining power and control over the relationship.

Social Learning Theory, Stress and Spouse Abuse

There is theoretical speculation that violence in the family results from a combination of stress factors in concert with one's behavioral repertoire. The application of social learning theory to spouse abuse begins with an individual's learning to respond violently to situations through modeling of the behavior of family members, peers and significant others. When stressor stimuli confront the batterer, he becomes frustrated and resorts to violence as an appropriate and justified action. Although this theory seems to present a compelling argument for family violence, some researchers argue that it is still not clear how the process of translating life events and stressors into violence actually takes place (Farrington, 1986). Why do some men abuse their wives and others not? A psychology of the individual and personality variables might serve to fill the gap between situational factors and differential responses.

One specific attempt to fill this gap has been the application of social learning theory to spouse abuse etiology through the study of intergenerational transmission of violence.

Data on intergenerational transmission of violence in relation to spouse abuse has been conflicting. Hofeller (1983) holds that nearly half of all men who batter their wives were either victims of physical abuse as children or observed violence perpetrated on their mothers by husbands or consorts and that, in general, violent men tend to come from dysfunctional families (in which relationships are strained due to the presence of alcoholism, drug-addiction, physical and sexual abuse and so on). Although this may indeed be so, Hofeller (1983) herself fails to support her speculations through empirical data.

Hotaling and Sugarman (1986) extracted 57 case-comparison studies from over 400 empirical reports on wife abuse to construct a list of "marker variables" (probable cause process indices) thought to be influential in spousal abuse. Risk markers were classified into one of four groups based on two criteria: the number of studies measuring the relationship between a risk marker and violence and the percentage of studies that supported the relationship between the risk marker and violence (p < .05).

Consistent risk markers were defined as those measured in three independent investigations and were supported in the results of the study. An inconsistent risk marker was defined as one which showed no consistent pattern across studies.

Two important findings emerged from the Hotaling and Sugarman (1986) study. *Witnessing parental violence* as a child or adolescent was found to be a *consistent risk marker*. *Experiencing physical abuse* as a child showed *inconsistency as a risk marker*.

Since violence against wives and exposure to parental violence as a child tend to be variables associated with males who engage in spouse abuse, it is unclear as to why experiencing physical abuse as a child does not show a consistent association with spouse abuse. However, experiencing physical abuse as a child has been shown to be associated with the greater likelihood that the individual will engage in abuse of his/her own offspring (Hotaling, Finkelhor, Kirkpatrick and Straus, 1988). Perhaps there is a tendency among people to perceive the modeling of significant others in terms of specific situations.

Another attempt to link multiple stressors and learning theory with marital aggression was made in a study by MacEwen and Barling (1988). Data were gathered from surveys completed by 275 couples. The hypothesis was that spouse abuse will only occur in response to stress when "aggression is in the behavioral and social repertoire of an individual." That is, when individuals have learned that violence is an appropriate and justified action in response to some situations, they will respond violently in response to some stressor stimuli.

But the results of the MacEwen and Barling (1988) study failed to show any significant effects for either the men or the women they sampled, perhaps because the sample was extracted from a larger sample of couples participating in a marital satisfaction study and few of the couples reported actual violence in their marriages.

Another study attempted to test the frustration-aggression theory in connection with social learning theory and its relation to spouse abuse. Howell and Pugliesi (1988) used a subsample of 960 males from a nationally stratified random sample of couples who self-reported violence. Though observing parental violence was found to be associated with marital violence, the frustration-aggression hypothesis was only minimally supported. Log-linear analysis (LOGIT) found main and interactive effects of age, occupational status, subjective economic strain and observation of parental violence. Employment status impacted on the strain of young men (which was determined by each individual's self-rating on a strain index); thus, young men in blue-collar occupations were more likely to report marital violence. One major limitation of the Howell and Puglieisi (1988) study was that only 19 percent of the total sample of males reported actually engaging in violence against their spouses. Further, this study only measured economic types of strain and did not seek to assess other types of strain which created frustration in the males.

Although observing or experiencing violence as a child and the likelihood of engaging in spousal violence is inconclusive, a new finding about a previous observation about the impact of dysfunctional families has emerged in recent empirical research.

Hamberger and Hastings (1988) found that those males who witnessed or experienced abuse as a child were more likely to engage in spousal violence *but*, experiencing or observing parental violence was *more characteristic of abusers with alcoholism problems*. Further, these abusers with alcoholism problems tend to come from dysfunctional families, more often from alcoholic and/or drug-abusing parents (Hamberger and Hastings, 1986; Schuerger and Reigle, 1988). This is consistent with clinical and observational reports (Hofeller, 1983).

The weight of the evidence seems to suggest that witnessing and experiencing violence in one's family of origin strongly increase the likelihood that an individual will engage in spouse abuse (Dutton, 1988). Further, dysfunctional families of origin, particularly ones where alcoholism or drug-addiction is prevalent, have a role in the intergenerational transmission of violence. Evidently, violent behaviors are not the only ones being transmitted through generations.

VIOLENCE GENERAL AND SPECIFIC

The psychosocial dimension has provided useful information about *who* the males are who engage in wife abuse.

Roberts (1987) profiled the psychosocial characteristics of a sample of 234 men who were brought into contact with a prosecutor's office on battering charges.

Batterers tended to be young, generally between the ages of 18 and 34 years old; 54% were white, while 44% were black; 47% unemployed; approximately 60% were intoxicated during the attack on their wives; 70% were under the influence of either alcohol and/or drugs; nearly 40% of the batterers had some form of prior criminal record.

A significant finding about judicial disposition also emerged from the study. Roberts (1987) found that, in slightly more than 60 percent of the cases, the charges were dropped or the case was dismissed. Only 3.9 percent of the batterers were incarcerated as a result of the battering charges. Consequently batterers, even though detected, go unsanctioned and very likely untreated with the opportunity to inflict bodily harm on their spouses once again.

Hotaling and Sugarman (1986) found that there is at least preliminary evidence regarding violent orientation in batterers. Specifically, batterers were found to report a greater likelihood of non-family violence than were non-batterers. This finding was specifically tested in a study by Shields, McCall and Henneke (1988). Using in-depth interviews, Shields, McCall and Henneke (1988) categorized 85 males on the basis of self-reported violence. The three categories included those individuals who used violence *only* in the familial setting, those individuals who reported using only non-familial violence and lastly, those males who reported as generally violent (including both family and nonfamily violence). Stepwise discriminant function analysis was used to determine which variables had the greatest explanatory powers in predicting patterns of violence. The generally violent group tended to use violence more frequently and more severely than either of the other groups. The family only violent group tended to be more law-abiding as well as less likely to be involved in extramarital relationships than either of the other two groups. The family-only violent individuals were also more likely to seek marital counseling than were the other groups, suggesting that the individual engaging in only family violence is truly interested in protecting and maintaining his relationship. Finally, the family-only violent male was more likely than either of the other two groups to have experienced violence as a child.

Thus it appears that there are patterns of male violence. Indeed, there is a greater likelihood that batterers will report more violence than non-batterers (Hotaling and Sugarman, 1986). Yet batterers themselves appear to be grouped into at least two discernible classes: (1) those who engage only in family violence and (2) those who engage in both family and non-family types of violence. At present batterers, by and large, cannot be characterized as demonstrating higher rates of non-family violence than non-batterers.

IMPLICATIONS FOR TREATMENT

Integrating theories of personality with social psychology pro-vides a clearer, more comprehensive view of the batterer in his social context (Kihlstrom, 1987). Each of three psychological per-spectives offered herein should not be viewed as mutually exclusive and exhaustive classifications. Rather, each contributes valuable in-formation about males who engage in spouse abuse and should be seen not only as complementary to each other, but also as part of the sociocultural atmosphere in which they are enmeshed.

From empirical research in the area of personality variables, males who engage in spouse abuse can be classified as having high rates of depression, dysphoria, anger-proneness, and to exhibit a high degree of histrionicity. Batterers tend to have distorted percep-tions of reality which border on schizoid/psychotic reactions to life events. This may explain why batterers show abnormally extreme jealousy over their partners as well as high rates of irrational thought and behavior.

The social learning perspective highlights a compelling argument of how violence may be transmitted from one generation to another. Multiple stressors on the individual appear to produce chronic frus-tration in the male, and, with his behavioral repertoire, he responds in what he believes is an appropriate and justified manner. For bat-terers, this means transferring externally derived frustration and an-ger onto the family setting, i.e., displacing anger and frustration onto an available and defenseless target (Toch, 1986). Addition-ally, the evidence indicates that not only are violent orientations intergenerationally transmitted, but other types of maladaptive cop-ing patterns (such as alcoholism and drug-addiction) may be trans-mitted from one generation to another as well and seem to be inti-mately linked to the problems of wife abuse.

Finally, the data offer a perspective about a number of character-istics of males who engage in spouse abuse. Generally, questions about the impact of employment, age, drug and alcohol use at the time of the attack on their wives all present some interesting facts about the batterer. By and large, batterers tend to be young and experience economic strain resulting from unemployment or low status blue-collar occupations.

In order to understand battering, it is necessary to look to the batterers themselves to comprehend the process of translating stressors and life events into acts of violence. As the population of spouse abusers is detected by the criminal justice system, researchers will be able to generate data about batterers by directly sampling the battering population.

Perhaps useful avenues of study in the future will test some of the general theories of violence and aggression, such as those offered by Hans Toch (1969) and Megargee and Hockanson (1970), who found that males find it more satisfying to elicit a counter-aggressive response when aggressed against. And females, contrarily, find it more satisfying to elicit a friendly response when aggressed against. It may be that, early in relationships characterized by violence, both partners elicit different responses to aggression. The men aggress against their partners, but the wives respond favorably or indifferently, but *not* aggressively. However, as the relationship continues and violence is utilized more frequently and/or more severely by the male against his wife, the wife gradually adopts a more aggressive stance and may even resort to violence as the relationship continues. This would seem to explain how the cycle of violence in some marriages is perpetuated and in fact, increases in severity and frequency as suggested by researchers (Justice Department Report, 1979; Stacey and Shupe, 1983).

One aspect not covered in the scope of this report is domestic violence consistency across situations. Toch (1986) seems to favor the idea of "contingent consistency," which implies a process of explaining the recurrence of violent behaviors across situations. The wife abuser establishes a predatory relationship with his wife, using a consistent approach to events. Toch (1986) suggests reviewing marital violence scenarios to dissect out of them recurrent situational and dispositional variables.

The situational variables are difficult to define in spouse abuse, primarily because the stimulus is often separated in time from the response. Thus, a noxious event may occur hours or days before the incident escalates and erupts into violence. As Toch (1986) put it:

Situational explanations often founder because the offender's motives are too idiosyncratic to be inferred. . . . Violent men have dispositions to react violently and these dispositions are triggered by a limited range of situations, in the sense that only some situations are disposition-relevant.

Toch seems to hold that as research develops in the area of males engaging in spouse abuse, more emphasis should be placed on the study of situational factors and focus on the scenario of the violent event itself.

REFERENCES

Adler, Freda. (1983). *Nations Not Obsessed with Crime*. Colorado: Fred B. Rothman & Company.

Audah, Abdul Karder. (1983). *Criminal Islamic Legislation: A Comparison with Positive Law*. Beirut, Lebanon. The Message Establishment.

Connick, Elizabeth. (1982). *The Experience of Women with Services for Abused Spouses in New York City*. New York: Victim Services Agency.

Dobash, R. and Dobash, Russell. (1979). *Violence Against Wives: A Case Against Patriarchy*. New York: The Free Press.

Dutton, Donald and Strachan, Catherine. (1987). Motivational Needs for Power. *Violence and Victims, V.2* (3).

Eddy, Melissa and Myers, Toby. (1984). *Helping Men who Batter: A profile of programs in the United States*. Texas: Texas Department of Human Resources.

Elbow, Margaret. (1977). Theoretical Considerations of Violent Marriages. *Social Casework*. November. 515-526.

Farrington, Keith. (1986). The Application of Stress Theory to the Study of Family Violence: Principles, Problems and Prospects. *Journal of Family Violence, V.1* (2). 131-146.

Ganley, Anne. (1981). *Court-mandated Counseling for Men who Batter: A Three-Day Workshop for Mental Health Professionals*. Washington, DC: Center for Women Policy Studies.

Gelles, Richard. (1976). Abused wives: Why do they stay? *Journal of Marriage and the Family*, 38 (November). 659-668.

Goolkasian, Gail. (1986). *Confronting Domestic Violence: The Role of Criminal Court Judges*. Washington, DC: National Institute of Justice.

Hamberger, Kevin L. and Hastings, James E. (1986). Personality Correlates of Men Who Abuse Their Partners: A Cross-Validation Study. *Journal of Family Violence, V.1* (4). 323-341.

Hamberger, Kevin L. and Hastings, James E. (1986). Characteristics of Spouse Abusers: Predictors of Treatment Acceptance. *Journal of Interpersonal Violence, V.1* (3) September. 363-373.

Hamberger, Kevin L. and Hastings, James E. (1988). Personality Characteristics of Spouse Abusers: A Controlled Comparison. *Violence and Victims, V.3* (1). 31-48.

Hofeller, Kathleen H. (1982). *Social, Psychological and Situational Factors in Wife Abuse*. California: R & E Research Associates.

Hofeller, Kathleen H. (1983). *Battered Women, Shattered Lives*. California: R & E Research Associates.

The Holy Qur'an: Text, Translation and Commentary. (1983). by A. Yusuf Ali. Maryland: Amana Corporation.

Hotaling, Gerald T. and Sugarman, David B. (1986). An Analysis of Risk Markers in Husband to Wife Violence: The Current State of Knowledge. *Violence and Victims, V.1* (2). 101-124.

Hotaling, Gerald T. and Finkelhor, Kirkpatrick and Straus. (1988). *Family Abuse and Its Consequences*. Calif.: Sage Publishing.

Howell, Marilyn J. (1988). Husbands Who Harm: Predicting Spousal Violence. *Journal of Family Violence, V.3* (1). 15-27.

Jennings, Jerry. (1987). History and Issues in the Treatment of Battering Men: A Case for Unstructured Group Therapy. *Journal of Family Violence, V.2* (3). 193-213.

Kalmuss, Debra and Straus, Murray. (1982). Wife's Marital Dependency and Wife Abuse. *Journal of Marriage and the Family, V.44* (2). 277-286.

Kalmuss, Debra. (1984). The Intergenerational Transmission of Marital Aggression. *Journal of Marriage and the Family, V.46* (1). 11-19.

Kihlstrom, John F. (1987). Introduction to the Special Issue: Integrating Personality and Social Psychology. *Journal of Personality and Social Psychology, V.53* (6). 989-992.

Levine, Edward M. (1986). Sociocultural Causes of Family Violence: A Theoretical Comment. *Journal of Family Violence, V.1* (1). 3-13.

MacEwen, Karyl E. and Barling, Julian. (1988). Multiple Stressors, Violence in the Family of Origin and Marital Aggression: A Longitudinal Investigation. *Journal of Family Violence, V.3* (1). 73-87.

Maiuro, Roland D., Cahn, Timothy S. and Vitaliano, Peter P. (1988). Anger, Hostility and Depression in Domestically Violent Versus Generally Assaultive Men and Nonviolent Control Subjects. *Journal of Consulting and Clinical Psychology, V.56* (1). 17-23.

Megargee, Edwin L. and Hockanson, Jack E. (1970). *The Dynamics of Aggression*. New York: Harper & Row Publishers.

Neidig, Peter H. and Friedman, Dale H. and Collins, Barbara S. (1986). Attitudinal Characteristics of Males Who Have Engaged in Spouse Abuse. *Journal of Family Violence, V.1* (3). 223-232.

Pagelow, Mildred. (1981). *Woman Battering: Victims and Their Experiences*. California: Sage Publications.

Roberts, Albert. (1987). Psychosocial Characteristics of Batterers: A Study of 234 men Charged With Domestic Violence Offenses. *Journal of Family Violence, V.2* (1). 81-93.

Rosenbaum, Alan. (1986). Of Men, Macho and Marital Violence. *Journal of Family Violence, V.1* (2). 121-129.

Roy, Maria. (1982). *The Abusive Partner: An Analysis of Domestic Battering.* New York: Van Nostrand Reinhold Co.

Schecter, Susan. (1982). *Women and Male Violence.* London: Pluto Press.

Shields, Nancy M., McCall, George J. and Henneke, Christine R. (1988). Patterns of Family and Nonfamily Violence: Husbands and Violent Men. *Violence and Victims, V.3* (2). 83-95.

Shuerger, J.M. and Reigle, N. (1988). Personality and Biographic Data That Characterize Men Who Abuse Their Wives. *Journal of Clinical Psychology, V.44* (1). 75-81.

Soler, Esta. (1987). Domestic Violence is a crime: A Case study—San Francisco Family Violence Project. In Sonkin, Daniel. *Domestic Violence on Trial: Psychological And Legal Dimensions of Family Violence.* New York: Springer Company.

Stacey, William and Shupe, Anson. (1983). *The Family Secret: Domestic Violence in America.* Mass.: Beacon Press.

Stacey, William and Shupe, Anson and Hazlewood, Lonnie. (1987). *Violent Men, Violent Couples.* Mass.: Lexington Books.

U.S. Department of Justice. (1979). *Special Report: Conference on Programs for Men Who Batter Women.* Washington, DC: Law Enforcement Association.

Toch, Hans. (1969). *Violent Men: An Inquiry into the Psychology of Violence.* Chicago: Aldine Publishing Company.

Toch, Hans. (1986). True to you, Darling, in My Fashion. In *Violent Transactions: The Limits of Personality.* Eds. Anne Cambell and John J. Gibbs. New York: Basil Blackwell.

Witt, David D. (1987). A Conflict Theory of Family Violence. *Journal of Family Violence, V.* 2(4). 291-300.

Men Who Abuse Their Spouses:
An Approach to Assessing Future Risk

Herbert R. Goldsmith

SUMMARY. Spouse abuse is a critical social issue in the United States. However, the literature is relatively silent on actual risk assessment for abuse cases. In the study described in this report, with a sample (N = 20) composed of abuse cases referred to a local spouse treatment center, a structured interview was developed from the research literature which addresses risk factors, focussing on the woman's perception of her mate's personality/behavioral characteristics, her perceptions of the relationship, and other situational factors associated with risk. The various types of abuse experienced were also documented. The majority of risk factors associated with spouse abuse as reported in the literature was confirmed in the sample. Utilizing the results of the study and the available literature, a pilot risk assessment instrument is presented, along with discussion of the efficacy of a standardized risk instrument.

Over 1.5 million women in the United States are assaulted by a male partner each year; a significant portion of these women will resort to killing their mate (Browne, 1987, pp.180-186). During 1984, one third of partner-related homicides involved women killing their husbands and two thirds husbands killing wives. Browne found that in cases which were at particularly high risk for a lethal incident (women kills in self-defense), the spouse could be identified by a cluster of reported factors, namely: frequency of assaultive incidents by the man; severity of injury; frequency of alcohol intox-

Herbert R. Goldsmith, CCMHC, served as coordinator of the project on alternative sentencing at the Harford County, Maryland, Sexual Assault and Spouse Abuse Resource Center. He is currently a senior caseworker with the State of Maryland's Juvenile Services Agency and at the Institute of Criminology and Criminal Justice at the University of Maryland, College Park.

45

ication or substance abuse by man; forced or threatened sexual assaults of the woman partner; the man's threats to kill; and suicide ideation by the woman. Browne believes these factors could be useful in identifying high-risk relationships in general, not just those in which the woman kills in self-defense. Assessment of risk in violent relationships via appropriate questioning should pay careful attention to the women's fears and perceptions of danger, keeping in mind interventions that do not assess significant risk factors can be iatrogenic and actually increase risk.

Denton (1988, p.19) summarized recent research on spouse abuse: that maritally violent men were reinforced in that behavior because it helped achieve dominion and sexual arousal followed the abuse; that most batterers felt suspicion of their wives and that their wives were responsible for the abuse, yet such men were also dependent on their wives for self-worth; that batterers frequently witnessed their fathers abusing their mothers or stepmothers; that alcohol abuse is associated with marital violence; that alcohol abuse frequently follows an incidence of abuse and may facilitate abuse but was not necessarily viewed as a cause.

Goolkasian (1986) reported that domestic violence occurs within all social, economic, ethnic, and religious groups. Hofeller (1952, pp.152-153), in an earlier extensive review of social, psychological, and situational factors in wife abuse, concluded that it was not possible to specify any one predisposing variable common to all battering; that dominance level was related to severity of violence; that physical force may be used as a means of achieving specific limited goals or may be used as achieving total dominion; and that personality factors should not be discounted but violence was best predicated by a combination of factors. These factors were violence backgrounds in both the man and the woman, status inequality, and heavy alcohol abuse by the man. Hofeller also found that women in the study felt community response was inadequate.

Browne (1987, p.168) reported, despite improvements in the criminal justice system's response to spouse abuse, many impediments still remain, such as the relative recency of the policies; policy inconsistencies across jurisdictions; entrenched negative attitudes; lack of formal arrests; and general lack of knowledge regarding risk elements by police and other members of the criminal justice system. Arrest itself was reported to be an appropriate response to certain abuse incidents (Sherman & Berk, 1984). State laws have recently expanded officers' legal authority to arrest in abuse cases in most states and police officer training addressing spouse abuse is beginning to be implemented (Goolkasian, 1986). For example, the state of Maryland recently enacted legislation allowing police officers to arrest a spouse abuser even if the officer did not witness the incident; however, there is evidence police may not be adequately trained in risk assessment and thus may make uninformed decisions. The officer may therefore arrest and detain an abuser of low risk or release a high risk subject. Personnel responsible for subsequent case decisions may also make uninformed decisions, and so on through the system, including those of judges, who play a critical role in shaping community response for those cases which enter the criminal justice system (Goolkasian, 1986). Regarding police, Garner and Clemmer (1986) found that the actual danger to police responding to abuse situations had generally been overstated.

Further, evidence of uniform policies for risk assessment across jurisdictions was lacking at the various levels within the criminal justice system. Perhaps recent legislation efforts have attempted to abate spouse abuse and have attempted to ameliorate sexism, but such efforts may have inadvertently left a void regarding appropriate implementation of the consequent laws and policies.

Utilizing descriptive research on a local sample and the information gleaned from the prior studies on the subject, the study described in this report addressed the following major issues: risk factors associated with spouse abusers; personality characteristics generally associated with the abuser; characteristics and risk factors associated with the abusive relationship; types of abuse committed; and generation of a risk assessment instrument.

With refinement and further research, a risk assessment instrument could prove to be valid, comprehensive, relatively simple to administer, reliable, and able to classify abusers into a risk category with reasonable accuracy. A refined instrument could be effectively utilized and field tested by clinicians, counselors, police officers, and other criminal justice personnel.

The risk instrument described in this report is considered a pilot and should only serve as an example or a model subject to modification, validation, and standardization based on the needs of the service delivery system involved and the needs of the affected population. For example, police officers may wish to use an abbreviated form which frequently utilizes scored closed ended questions, whereas clinicians may wish to utilize a longer form which frequently uses open ended questions.

The following terms are clarified for this report. *Spouse abuse* generally refers to assaultive behavior involving couples who are married, cohabitating, or have an ongoing or prior intimate relationship. *Status inequality* refers to the socio-economic level of the woman's family being significantly higher than the socio-economic level of the batterer's family. *Cycles of abuse* refers to the building up of tension within the abuser and the relationship, the subsequent release of hostility/tension via an abuse incident, the period of contrition that often follows and the subsequent period of tranquillity generally known as the "honeymoon period." Tension once again builds up and the cycle is repeated. The remainder of the terms are self explanatory or defined within the text.

METHOD

Subjects

Twenty spouse abuse cases were selected by "the convenience of being available." The sample consisted of couples referred to a local spouse abuse/sexual assault resource center for treatment. The couples or abuser were referred as follows: court (N = 3); spouse (N = 14); hospital (N = 2); and therapist (N = 1). Each case was examined via a structured interview with the abused spouse by the author at the normally scheduled intake interview. All subjects were processed and researched in the order they were referred during calendar year 1985. All cases were married and cohabitating together, or were married and temporarily separated due to an abuse incident. The clients were white males with an age range of 18 to 53 years. Formal education ranged from completion of 8th grade to attainment of a bachelor's degree.

Procedure

The abused spouses were interviewed via a structured format facilitated by a standardized paper and pencil instrument constructed from relevant research literature. The interview was designed to detect the presence of the personality characteristics often associated with abusers, the presence of characteristics often associated with abusive relationships, situational risk factors, and was designed to detect the various types of abuse that occurred for each case. All interviews were conducted prior to initiation of formal treatment.

RESULTS

Table 1 illustrates the various abuser characteristics as perceived by the abused spouse. The results indicate that dominance, anger, blaming, minimization, poor self-image, moodiness, acceptance of violence as a problem solving technique, alcohol/substance abuse, possible emotional disturbance, rigid cognitive styles, and jealousy were perceived in at least 75% of the relationships (N $\geq$ 15). Less than 50% of the spouses reported their husbands had been abused or had witnessed abuse of their mother/female guardian.

Table 2 illustrates the characteristics of the relationship as perceived by the abused spouse. The results indicated cycles of abuse, lack of communication, and fear of divorce were present in at least 85% of the cases (N $\geq$ 17). Sixty percent (60%) reported sexual problems, unrealistic expectations, and problems with children. Financial problems and the wife having significantly more formal education were reported in 55% of the cases, and an excess of traditional values was reported in 50% of the cases. Status inequality was reported in less than 40% of the cases.

The types of abuse reported and the percentage of spouses reporting that type of abuse were: physical abuse (100%); psychological/emotional abuse (90%); destruction of property and/or harm to pets (85%); and sexual abuse (30%), which included forced sex, rape, etc. Table 3 presents details.

Table 1:   Reported Characteristics of the Abusers

Characteristic	No. of Spouses/ Mates Reporting
Violent when angered	19
Prone to blaming others or things for his problems	19
Domineering or control oriented	18
Easily angered	18
Acceptance of violence as a problem solving technique	18
Minimization of the abuse incident(s)	18
Insecure and poor self image	17
Charming and friendly w/others	17
Moody	17
Minimization of emotional problems	17
Jealous	16
Heavy drinker and/or drug abuser	16
Attempted to conform spouse to his standard	15
Dr. Jekyl and Mr. Hyde persona	15
Cycles of depression	15
Rigid thinking patterns	15
Rigid gender roles	15
Macho type behavior	14
Impulsive	14
Selfish	13
A bully	13
External locus of control	13
Muscle Tension	12
Apathetic	11
Poor communication skills	11
Abusive in the courtship	11
Self-imposed isolation	10
Reduced awareness of feelings (e.g.,only shows anger)	10
Normally a hostile/violent personality type	9
Only intimate for sex	9
A person who was abused as a child	9
A person who witnessed abuse of his mother	7
Cruel to animals	7
Mentally ill, crazy, or disturbed	6
Preoccupied with weapons	6
Unemployed a great deal	5
Prone to police arrests	5
Suicidal	4
Poor in social skills	4
Afraid of intimacy	3

Note: N=20

DISCUSSION

The results indicated that at least 75% of the sample confirmed the presence of several well known and documented risk factors associated with the abuser and the abusive relationship. In general, these factors related to dominance, the presence of various types of abuse, alcohol/drug abuse, family/marital tension, possible emo-

Table 2: Reported Characteristics of the Abusive Relationships

Characteristics	No. of Spouses/ Mates Reporting
Cycles of abuse (violent act, honeymoon period,...)	18
Lack of communication	18
Fear of divorce	17
Problems with the children	12
Sexual difficulties	12
Unrealistic expectations	12
Financial problems	11
Wife had significantly more formal education	11
Excess of traditional values	10
Rigid sex roles	8
Problems with health	8
Status inequality (wife from a "better home")	7
Problems with employment	6

Note: N=20

Table 3: Reported Types of Abuse

Types of Abuse	No. of Spouses/ Mates Reporting
Physical abuse upon spouse	20
Psychological abuse upon spouse	18
Destruction of property and/or harm to pets	17
Sexual abuse (forced sex, etc.)	6

Note: N=20

tional disturbance, and the use of physical force to achieve and maintain dominance. Status inequality (35%), violence in the abuser's (40%) or spouse's (55%) background was reported relatively less frequently.

The literature and this study suggest it may be practical and tenable to rely on actual behavioral/personality characteristics perceived by the abused spouse, in conjunction with certain situational factors, for risk assessment/screening; actual case treatment would probably also benefit from analysis of social and historical factors. Browne, as cited previously, felt that the wife's fears and perception of danger are significant risk factors. Many of the fears will most likely be revealed or reported in the wife's appraisal of the abuser's personality/behavioral characteristics, as well as her appraisal of the relationship and current situation. For example, a fear of divorce may be substantially influenced by a fear of abuser retribution if a formal separation were actively sought. Nevertheless, an actual risk assessment instrument would aid in organizing valid risk factors for assessment and decision making.

Instruments derived from statistical and actuarial measurements have shown to be of value for determining appropriate supervision levels for criminal probationers based on assessment of risk (U.S. National Institute of Corrections, 1979). The instruments are typically written forms containing a fixed set of weighted criteria, which are combined into an overall offender summary score. The benefits reported were: applicability as a screening tool, case screening expedition, and common vocabulary for case discussion. Despite some inherent problems with statistically generated instruments (lack of validation, low predictive accuracy, poorly designed research), the U.S. National Institute of Corrections reported that judicious use of validated instruments could have clear advantages, such as: documented and discernible decision criteria, probable equitable treatment as a result of consistency in decision making, and increased decision accuracy as contrasted to the accuracy of purely subjective decisions. Wright, Clear and Dickson (1984) researched risk screening devices for probationers and felt such instruments should be promoted; however, they also believe that instruments should be validated locally.

Screening tools based on statistical measures for abuse risk assessment would be a distinct asset for both the counseling and criminal justice community. Such tools would help alleviate some of the impediments Browne has cited; risk assessment instruments would provide immediate risk assessment knowledge and provide a mechanism for policy/procedure standardization. Risk instruments would aid police officers with their case decisions, including emergency situations, and provide officer managers with a police officer training aid. Clinicians, on the other hand, may feel more secure treating cases after a structured risk assessment, especially if reporting to a court is required. The criminal justice community and the courts would obviously benefit from the more objectively generated risk assessments. Organizations and agencies affiliated with the treatment of spouse abuse would probably benefit from the resultant standardization and continuity which would accompany the proposed risk assessments.

Risk assessment instruments also provide: capability of workload management; data for information systems; and provide a mechanism for resource allocations and program needs analysis. Workload management would be better gauged as a result of a caseload being differentiated by risk. Caseloads delineated by various levels of risk provide a better descriptive measure and workload indicator than caseloads described by a single number indicating the existent number of cases. Objective risk categorization also generates valuable data for information systems and, as a result, would provide measures for resource needs and provide information for resource allocations. For example, there are strong indications a significant number of abusers would profit from a formal psychological evaluation, but such services are often costly or not readily available. A risk instrument would help prioritize which cases receive this service.

Further research is needed for the generation of reliable/valid risk instruments, the generation of norm derivations of such instruments for the effected populations, and, most importantly, to determine the viability of spouse abuse risk assessment instruments. Figure 1 illustrates a prospective risk assessment instrument design. Part I of the instrument would probably be of interest to law enforcement personnel, with Part II providing the capability to provide further relevant risk data if time and/or the situation allows for a more in depth inquiry.

Regardless, clinicians would probably be interested in both parts, coupled with further clinical inguiry. The proposed model suggests low, moderate, and high levels of risk assessment. The assignment of a level to a case would depend on the derived score range; for example, a score that falls within a range of 0-15 for Part I, or 0-25 for Parts I and II combined, may be considered a low risk case. It is to be emphasized that any instrument needs to be field tested and researched for its validity/reliability before any actual score ranges could be utilized; local norms also should be formulated.

Figure 1: Suggested Model for Spouse Abuse Risk Assessment/Screening

Abuser's Name: _____ DOB/Age _____ Race _____

Spouse's Name: _____ DOB/Age _____ Race _____

Person Filling Out Form: _____ Title: _____ Date: _____

Part I

Check one ( ) per item, except for item 9, and enter the corresponding number in the
[ ] by each main heading. Place 0 in the [ ] if the answer is none, if that item
does not apply, or if none of the given responses apply.

1. Current Abuse Incident.....( )...[ ]
   a. No visible marks,   ( ) 1
   b. Bruises, contusions,   ( ) 5
      abrasions, cuts not
      requiring sutures
   c. Broken bones and/or   ( ) 7
      cuts requiring sutures

2. Frequency of Abuse.........( )...[ ]
   a. Once a year   ( ) 2
   b. Twice a year   ( ) 4
   c. Three times a year   ( ) 6
   d. More than three times   ( ) 8
      a year

3. Severest Past Abuse Incident....( )..[ ]
   a. No visible marks,   ( ) 1
   b. Bruises, contusions,   ( ) 5
      abrasions, cuts not
      requiring sutures
   c. Broken bones and/or   ( ) 7
      cuts requiring sutures

4. Length of Abuse...........( )...[ ]
   a. 1 year   ( ) 1
   b. 2 - 3 years   ( ) 3
   c. Over 4 years   ( ) 5

5. Forced Sexual Acts.........( )...[ ]
   (during last year)
   a. Once   ( ) 2
   b. Twice   ( ) 4
   c. More than twice   ( ) 6

6. Frequency of Alcohol Abuse....( )..[ ]
   a. Once every 3 months   ( ) 1
   b. Once a month   ( ) 3
   c. More than once a month   ( ) 5

7. Frequency of Drug Abuse.....( )..[ ]
   a. Once every 3 months   ( ) 1
   b. Once a month   ( ) 3
   c. More than once a month   ( ) 5

8. Wife's Level of Fear.......( )..[ ]
   a. Minimum amount reported   ( ) 1
      or displayed
   b. Moderate amount reported ( ) 3
      or displayed
   c. Considerable amount re-   ( ) 5
      ported or displayed

9. Type of Abuse in Last Year....( )..[ ]
   (check and score all that apply)
   a. Physical   ( ) 3
   b. Psychological/Emotional   ( ) 2
   c. Sexual   ( ) 3
   d. Harm to property or pets ( ) 2

****
*** SCORING FOR PART I
****
*** Sum of 1 - 9 (range= 0 - 58)
****
*** RISK ASSESSMENT BASED ON PART I ONLY
*** (check one only)
****
*** Low   Moderate   High
****

54

```
*****************************************************
Part II
For the following items, circle 2 if the item is very true or often true; circle 1
if the item is somewhat or sometimes true; or circle 0 if is not true or not relevant.

   0 = Not True    1 = Somewhat or Sometimes True    2 = Very True or Often True


                                                                    PART II SCORE _____

0  1  2   10. Victim has seriously contemplated suicide
0  1  2   11. Victim has attempted suicide
0  1  2   12. Abuser has seriously contemplated suicide
0  1  2   13. Abuser has attempted suicide
0  1  2   14. Abuser is jealous/suspicious of wife
0  1  2   15. Abuser is easily angered
0  1  2   16. Abuser is abusive when angered
0  1  2   17. Abuser blames wife for abuse incident(s)
0  1  2   18. Abuser is seeking control/dominion over wife
0  1  2   19. Abuser uses violence to gain or retain dominion over wife
0  1  2   20. Abuser threatens to sexually assault wife
0  1  2   21. Abuser minimizes the abuse incidents
0  1  2   22. Abuser threatens to kill wife
0  1  2   23. Cycles of violence is present in relationship
0  1  2   24. Abuser is moody

SCORING FOR PARTS I&II COMBINED      RISK ASSESSMENT FOR PARTS I&II COMBINED
Sum of Part I ( range= 0 - 58)____   ____Low  ____Moderate  ____High
Sum of Part II ( range= 0 - 30)____         Comments:_____
Total Sum ( range= 0 - 88)____              _____

Note: Actual Risk Assessment levels would be based on assigned score level ranges
```

REFERENCES

Browne, A. *When battered women kill.* New York: The Free Press, 1987.

Denton, L. Batterers reinforced by increased control. *APA Monitor*, August 1987, p. 19; 8.

Garner, J. & Clemmer, E. Danger to police in domestic disturbances—a new look. *Research in Brief* (Washington, DC: National Institute of Justice, November 1986).

Goolkasian, G. A. Confronting domestic violence: the role of criminal court judges. *Research in Brief* (Washington, DC: National Institute of Justice, November 1986).

Hofeller, K. H. *Social, psychological and situational factors in wife abuse.* Palo Alto, Ca.: R & E Research Associates, 1982.

Sherman, L.W. & Berk, R.A. The specific deterrent effects of arrest for domestic assault. *American Sociological Review*, 1984, *49*, 261-272.

U.S. National Institute of Corrections. *Classification instruments for criminal justice decisions* (Vol. 2). Washington, DC: The National Council on Crime and Delinquency, 1979.

Wright, K.N., Clear, T.R., & Dickson, P. Universal applicability of probation risk-assessment instruments. Criminology, 1984, *22* (1), 113-134.

Treating Abusive Parents
in Outpatient Settings

Mary L. Otto

SUMMARY. Many abusive parents were victims of child abuse. Their normal cycle of development was interrupted by conflict and trauma leaving them unable to make normal adult adjustments to the role of parent. This outpatient treatment model describes a psychoeducational approach to helping abusive parents acquire skills that are absent as a result of deficits in their childhood development.

Child abuse has been well-documented as a serious, but somewhat improving problem for children and their families. Murray and Gelles (1986) report that even though the rate of reported child abuse has decreased in the past ten years, the incidence of child abuse remains extremely high. Newspapers, magazines, and professional journals abound with information about and suggestions for resolving the problems of child abuse. The attention given to child abuse makes it clear that this is not just a problem for the involved family. Child abuse is in the forefront of society's unresolved problems. Abused children frequently become adults with serious emotional and behavioral problems such as multiple personality syndrome (Coons, 1986), spouse abuse (Hamberger & Hastings, 1986), and child abuse (Ney, 1987).

Abused children are often unable to adjust socially or academically in school. Their sense of isolation and powerlessness forces many young teenagers to run away from home to escape from their family and search for a sense of control. Life on the street has serious negative consequences for these individuals, such as prostitu-

Mary L. Otto, PhD, is Associate Professor and Director of Research and Academic Development at Oakland University.

tion (McMullen, 1986). Runaways living on the street usually die young. Reports suggest that as many as 5,000 teenagers a year are buried in unmarked graves (Newsweek, 1988). Those who do survive are seldom able to avoid the lifestyle of street drugs, prostitution and violence.

All types of child abuse present concern for the child, the family and society. However, all abuse is not the same. Abusive behavior is expressed as sexual, physical and psychological abuse and is manifested in degrees of seriousness. It exists on a continuum from severe to less severe or marginal.

Usually severe abuse is more easily defined because the behavior and results are visible. Severe abuse results in obvious physical damage threatening the child's physical health and often his/her life. Less severe or marginal abuse is more difficult to determine because the results are not so specific. Halperin (1979) defines marginal abuse as hindering the child's growth. Since the impact of severe, life-threatening abuse is observable, it is also clear that children have a right to protection. However, many abuse situations are not classified as severe. These cases do not demand the intervention of authorities or protective services; yet, this type of child abuse may very well contribute to creating a population of teenage runaways and young adults who are likely to perpetuate child abuse into the next generation.

Abused children respond to their childhood trauma in many ways; one of these is identifying with the aggression (Ney, 1987). Without treatment, they generally become insecure, isolated adults who are unable to support a positive relationship. Although abusive parents are viewed as willful, evil villains inflicting harm on innocent children, the generational pattern of reoccurrence in violent families suggests that abusive parents, themselves, are also victims. In spite of the attempts to educate society about child abuse, stories about abuse directed at a child continue to illicit angry and even violent reactions toward abusive parents.

Abusive parents are considered deviant although there is overwhelming evidence that child abuse is not uncommon (Gil, 1974). Viewing abusive parents as deviant leads to criticism and threatening ultimatums rather than a provision for support and help from the community. Abusive parents are not likely to seek help if they fear being chastised or loosing their children. In effect the system, by responding negatively, has made it difficult for abusive parents to ask for help. Thus, the sense of isolation is perpetuated. With regard to alleviating the problems of child abuse, it is important to understand that abusive parents are not monsters who deserve punishment, but victims of their own unresolved childhood trauma.

While some abusive parents report feelings of discomfort with their violent behavior and anger toward their children, many others do not realize their violence is a problem until a child is seriously injured or they are involved in a review mandated by the court. Treatment, then, must be supportive to ease the fear and discomfort and educational to teach the impact of child abuse. The model presented is psychoeducational providing an educational approach to teach psychological skills that are absent as a result of deficits in earlier developmental stages.

OUTPATIENT TREATMENT

Treating an abusive parent in an outpatient setting allows the parent to begin integrating new ideas and behaviors into a daily routine from the beginning of treatment. This is important because the change must be made and maintained in the abusive parent's environment with all its stresses and problems present. It also allows the parent to try out new behaviors, discuss the outcomes and receive feedback about making alterations.

This psychoeducational outpatient treatment model focuses on a teaching/learning approach for working with abusive parents. The model contains a parent education component to help parents learn about the relationship between developmental stages and related behaviors. This part of the treatment is aimed at defining behaviors in children that might stimulate the abusive parent to aggression even though the behavior is normal and appropriate for the child's developmental stage. The educational component also provides information about family violence so that abusive parents can begin to understand how their childhood experience affected them and that the cycle will continue if it's not interrupted by behavior change.

The model also includes group counseling to help abusive parents understand their personal problems and manage their emotional relationship with their children. Since abusive parents have been cited (Helfer & Kempe, 1976; Starr, 1982) as suffering from isolation, this treatment model relies on group interaction to alleviate the sense of isolation and provide support. The educational component is delivered to a group of abusive parents who remain together in group counseling to process the information. Involvement with a group of adults who have similar problems gives them an opportunity to interact responsibly with other people. Over time the parents are able to explore their fears, frustrations, anger and other feelings.

Individual counseling should be available for those parents who exhibit emotional problems that cannot be properly addressed by only group counseling. For example, individual counseling may be added for parents whose depression requires extra help. This treatment option should also be available for abusive parents with multiple personality syndrome or borderline personality traits. These individuals would not be good candidates for group counseling, but might benefit from individual counseling.

Because all types of abuse, physical, psychological and sexual, affect the entire family, treatment should be available for all family members. All children in the same family may not be direct victims of abusive behavior, but they witness the traumatic interaction between their brother or sister and the parent. This violent behavior in the family leads to maladjusted responses and interpersonal problems. The children need help to alleviate their sense of guilt. When there are two adults in the home, one adult is often the active abuser and the other passively condones the behavior. The adult who passively supports abuse needs to understand his/her role and learn how to support non-abusive behavior. Whenever possible, treatment for the less involved family members should be concurrent with treatment for the abusive parent and the victim.

Treatment for the abuse victim is very important. Although treating the abusive parent will alleviate future abuse, the abuse victim will already have serious problems that must be addressed. The style of treatment for the victim will depend on the type and length of abuse. Short-term treatment can be effective with the nonchronically abused, but in cases of chronic abuse a combination of long-term, insight-oriented treatment and support programs is recommended (Mouzakitis, 1984).

Working with abusive parents requires knowledge about treatment models for child abuse (Gelardo & Sanford, 1987), developmental stages of adults and children and associated behaviors, and effective parenting strategies that are theoretically sound and reflect realistic living conditions. It also requires well-developed teaching and counseling skills. But, most importantly, it requires an understanding of the abusive parent. Abusive parents need acceptance and support to integrate what they learn through treatment. This model can be implemented by one counselor, but it is best delivered through the collaborative efforts of two counselors. One counselor assumes responsibility for making the classroom-type presentations to the parents and the other for leading the group interaction. Both counselors should be parents so they can relate to the parenting issues from an experiential as well as theoretical base.

Since the specific treatment needs of abusive parents are varied, this psychoeducational model should be viewed as a method that will work with some but not all abusive parents. Group counseling and presentations are major components of the model, so abusive parents should be screened for the responsiveness to both methods. For example, parents who participate in this treatment plan must be able to attend to others and listen to presentations for up to twenty minutes. It is an ideal treatment for abusive parents who, although unable to parent without violence, have the capability of learning and the desire to implement adaptive, non-violent parenting behaviors. It works with parents who begin treatment reluctantly as well as those who request treatment.

Time lines cannot be strictly enforced because each group of parents who enter this program will move through treatment at different rates. Successful response to treatment can be severely limited by demanding that abusive parents learn and change on a tightly prescribed schedule. The following time estimates are based on experience with the model and can be used only as a guide. With each session lasting 2 hours, including presentation time, Phase I takes 3-5 sessions, Phase II 5-7 sessions, Phase III 3-5 sessions, and closure 1-2 sessions.

REFERENCES

Coons, P.M. Child Abuse and Multiple Personality Disorder: Review of the Literature and Suggestions For Treatment, *Child Abuse & Neglect*, 1986 *10(4)* 455-462.

Gelardo, M.S. & Sanford, E.E. Child Abuse and Neglect: A Review of the Literature, *The School Psychology Review*, 1987, *16(21)*, 137-155.

Gil, D. A Conceptual Model of Child Abuse and its Implications for Social Policy in Steinmetz, S. & Straus, M. (Eds.), *Violence in the Family*, New York: Harper & Row, 1974.

Halperin, Michael. *Helping Maltreated Children: School and Community Involvement*, St. Louis: C.V. Mosby, 1979.

Hamberger, L.K. & Hastings, J.E. Characteristics of Spouse Abusers: Predictors of Treatment Acceptance, *Journal of Interpersonal Violence*, 1986, *1(3)* 363-373.

Helfer, R.E. & Kempe, C.H. *Child Abuse and Neglect: The Family and the Community*, Cambridge, Mass.: Bollinger, 1976.

McMullen, R.J. Youth Prostitution: A Balance of Power? *International Journal of Offender Therapy & Comparative Criminology*, 1986, *30(3)*, 237-244.

Mouzakitis, C.M. Characteristics of Abused Adolescents and Guidelines for Intervention, *Child Welfare*, 1984, *63(2)* 149-157.

Ney, P.G. The Treatment of Abused Children: The Natural Sequence of Events, *American Journal of Psychotherapy*, 1987, *41(3)*, 391-401.

Starr, R.H. A Research-based Approach to the Prediction of Child Abuse in Starr, R. (ed.) *Child Abuse Prediction: Policy Implications*, Cambridge, Mass.: Bollinger Publishing, 1982.

Straus, M.A. & Gelles, R.J. Societal change and change in family violence from 1975 to 1985 as revealed in two national surveys, *Journal of Marriage & the Family*, 1986, *48(3)*, 465-479.

APPENDIX
Out Patient Treatment

Phase I

Goals for Abusive Parents

A. Stop physical abuse

Because physical abuse is threatening to the child's welfare and easily defined for the parent, it is the focus of the first behavior change.

B. Make a commitment to treatment

Although the parents do not have to agree with the premise that their behavior is unacceptable, they do have to agree to participate in the complete treatment program.

Intervention Strategies

Presentation Topics

Begin each session with a twenty minute presentation about family violence. Discuss the frequency of family violence and then move to specific information about child abuse, including information about inter-generational reoccurrence.

Group Counseling

Each member is asked to describe their current abuse situation. The focus is on the present with little reference to past experiences.

Phase II

A. Learn new parenting strategies.

When parents agree to stop hitting, new behaviors must replace the violence.

B. To control their behavior.

By engaging in new behaviors, and not reverting to violence, abusive parents begin to discuss abilities rather than focusing only on weaknesses.

Presentation Topics

Describe various successful strategies for resolving conflict and encouraging cooperation. Also explain that children do not always welcome behavior change. (A child who has learned to cope with abuse, will attempt to push the parent into violence.)

Present information about children not being to blame for what happens to them.

Group Counseling

Members discuss their experiences with new behaviors, frustrations with their children. They also begin to understand that they, too, were helpless victims as children.

Phase III

Goals for Abusive Parents

A. Self-acceptance

As the parents establish supportive relationships with group members, they are able to recognize positive attributes in themselves.

B. Self-understanding

The participants begin to understand that these childhood experiences affected their adult behavior. They can now make appropriate decisions as parents because they have acquired .
knowledge about how to parent.

Intervention Strategies

Presentation topics

Session begins with a presentation about personal growth topics such as goal setting, asking for help, and helping others. When appropriate, adult developmental stages and the related needs also can be presented.

Group Counseling

Members discuss their feelings about themselves. Since abusive parents have very low self-esteem, it is important to move slowly. The parents accept responsibility for their behavior rather than blaming others.

Phase IV
(closure)

A. Make plans for additional counseling or education

Many parents will still need counseling and some will want more education about parenting and self growth.

B. Establish a support system

The parents will need a support system to maintain behavior changes.

Presentation topics

Present specific information about community college, university or night school courses and provide referral information for counseling.

Provide information on support groups such as Parents Anonymous.

Group Counseling

Discuss plans for support and exchange phone numbers. Review the difficulty of maintaining behavior change so parents will not be inappropriately discouraged.

Treatment Needs and Services for Mothers with a Dual Diagnosis: Substance Abuse and Mental Illness

Sylvia K. Morris
Steven P. Schinke

SUMMARY. Women who are diagnosed as substance abusers and as mentally ill are at risk for psychosocial, legal, and economic problems. When these women are mothers, the challenges they and their children face are evermore serious. This paper reviews the treatment needs of dual diagnosed, substance abusing and mentally ill mothers. Next, the paper suggests treatment strategies and programmatic options for comprehensively serving and meeting the needs of these mothers and their children. Particular attention is devoted to the promise of residential and continuing care services and skills based interventions for the target clients. After describing research methods suitable to the evaluation of the recommended human services, the paper concludes with an agenda for further investigations of the needs and appropriate services for dual diagnosed mothers with a history of substance abuse and mental illness.

Investigators and clinicians in many human services fields are challenged by client populations who defy facile diagnostic labels and categories. Not only do the members of these populations elude the unambiguous descriptors and labels of an earlier, perhaps more naive era, but what is more, such clients demand a new, evermore complex array of treatment and programmatic services. Hence, researchers and practitioners from such fields as substance abuse treatment, mental health services, criminal justice, social work, and

Sylvia K. Morris is at the Project Return Foundation, 133 West 21st Street, New York, NY 10011.

Steven P. Schinke, PhD, is Professor of Social Work at Columbia University.

The authors acknowledge the assistance of Janet Lerner in the literature search and Kristen Cole in the preparation of this manuscript.

public welfare are less likely than ever before to be afforded the luxury of studying and working with clients who fall neatly within one exclusive diagnostic category.

Among the most complex groups of clients who are not described by a single diagnostic term are those with a history of substance abuse and mental illness. In this paper, we focus on the treatment needs of a subset of those clients. Specifically, the paper details the special circumstances that surround women who are mothers and who also have a history of substance abuse and mental illness.

Toward adding new knowledge to the newly recognized and emerging area of dual diagnosed substance abusing and mentally ill mothers and due to space limitations, the paper does not purport to give a comprehensive and exhaustive discussion of the myriad issues involved in substance abuse and mental health treatment. Rather, we have limited our discussion to those salient issues that have yet to capture wide scientific and professional attention in understanding and serving members of the target population.

BACKGROUND

In the state of New York, female substance abusers numbered 671,500 at last count (New York State Department of Substance Abuse Services, 1983). Of these women, between 60% and 70% are estimated to have children (Sutker, 1981). Only one out of every 23 women in New York state who is a diagnosed substance abuser is receiving treatment (New York State Department of Substance Abuse Services, 1981). Few substance abuse or mental health programs include children in their mother's treatments; even fewer programs address substance abuse and mental health issues concurrently; virtually no existing programs simultaneously address substance abuse problems, mental illness, and child management issues among women and mothers.

TREATMENT NEEDS

Women who are mothers and who are mentally ill present multiple concerns for human services providers and programs. Substance abusers of either gender have medical, emotional, interpersonal, legal, educational, and vocational difficulties. The family problems of these clients may further exacerbate and interfere with treatment (Eldred, Grier, & Berliner, 1974). As such, comprehensive care may be necessary to meet the extensive needs of substance abusing, mentally ill mothers and their children (Eldred et al., 1974).

From empirical research come findings that addicted mothers performed less adaptively on measures of personality and parenting behavior (Bauman & Dougherty, 1983). The mothers in this study reflected such characteristics as impulsivity, irresponsibility, immaturity, and self-centeredness. Perhaps confounding these data are other findings to suggest that, as children, drug dependent women have experienced a greater incidence of rape, incest, neglect and abuse than nonaddictive women experienced as children (Mondanaro, Wedenoja, Densen-Gerber, Elahi, Mason, & Redmond, 1982).

Mothers who abuse drugs and who are mentally ill are themselves at risk for child abuse and neglect. Relative to nonaddicted mothers, addicted mothers are more demanding of their children and less likely to allow children to proceed with the individuation process (Wellisch & Steinberg, 1980). As such, parental drug addiction is a predominant characteristic for neglect and emotional deprivation of children (Billing, Eriksson, Larsson, & Zellerstrom, 1979).

Expectedly, women who abuse drugs are neither ideal mothers nor are they apt to provide optimal role models for their children. These mothers inadvertently model deviancies that their children may later manifest as drug use or as delinquency (Elliott, Huizinga, & Ageton, 1985; Hawkins, Lishner, & Catalano, 1985). Parental modeling is also a potent contributor to children's later use of cigarettes, alcohol, and illicit use of prescription drugs (Fawzy, Coombs, & Gerber, 1983; Needle, Glynn, & Needle, 1983).

Indeed, children of drug abusing women tend to exhibit such characteristics as hyperactivity, flat affect, and promiscuous attachment (Billing et al., 1979; Bauman & Dougherty, 1983). Possibly, the high levels of coercion that frequently mark the interactions of addicted mothers and their children serve as chronic events that can lead to child abuse and neglect (cf. Loeber & Tengs, 1986; Schindler & Arkowitz, 1986).

Children's emotional and character development are likely affected by maternal substance use. In support of this tenet, studies on attachment show a relationship between maternal deprivation and children's development of anti-social personality characteristics (Bowlby, 1966). Along a parallel track, in defining the antisocial personality disorder among children, Rowe (1981) noted that parental role models have a salient effect on children's development of antisocial characteristics. Children of substance abusers are therefore candidates for school failure, social incompetence, slowed intellectual and emotional growth, and associated difficulties later in life.

Children who do not bond to mothers—possibly due to physical and emotional separation—do not develop adaptive character traits. Maternal deprivation has frequently been found in the mother-child relationship where substance abuse is a prominent behavior of the mother (Eldred et al., 1974). Without intervention, children may be doomed to repeat their mother's substance abuse and anti-social behaviors.

POTENTIAL FOR TREATMENT

Parenting Awareness

Fortunately, one of the factors that may motivate women to seek help for their substance abuse problem is the realization that they are not providing the parenting they want for their children. Addicted women may begin their parenting careers with a sense of guilt and failure. The demands of their addictions then interfere with the mothering process. At some point, these women inevitably face interruption of their mothering role due to arrest, hospitalization or intervention from child welfare. Consequently, addicted mothers may seek treatment when faced with the threat of termination of their parental rights.

Data reported by Rosenbaum (1979) suggest that addicted mothers see motherhood as their purpose in life. These women defined their femininity by the effectiveness with which they meet this responsibility. Other findings indicate that substance abusing women can, with parent education for example, improve as parents (Pearlman et al., 1982). Many of these women have developed insight into the negative effects of their own upbringing and have resolved to prevent similar problems for their children.

Subsequently, mothers may begin to develop their own sense of basic trust and foster similar growth in their children. Mothers can then learn how to gear interactions with children to the appropriate developmental level. Parent education and concomitant improvement of the parent-child relationship has facilitated integration of substance abuse treatment. As a result, recovery time has been shortened by mothers' increased sense of competency as a parent (Lief, 1981).

The parenting concerns of dual diagnosed mothers, therefore, can be a strength and foundation for subsequent treatment efforts. Effective interventions must then advance this strength and build on mothers' parenting awareness. When parenting competence is lacking, treatment programs and individual intervention efforts should assume the mother's desire to improve her competence exists. This assumption should give treatment providers more optimism than pessimism for mothers' eventual therapeutic improvement.

Psychosocial Supports

Added strengths for building effective treatment programs to meet the needs to women who have a history of substance abuse and mental illness come from extant or potential psychosocial supports. An early descriptive study by Tucker (1979) found differences in the social supports of women who were addicted to heroin relative to women who were drug free. In particular, Tucker reported:

> Addicted women were more likely than . . . [nonaddicted] women but as likely as addicted men to exchange practical rather than emotional support with best friends. The addicted women are particularly dependent on their mothers for child-rearing support and, to a lesser extend, financial aid. (p. 71)

Also in early research, Colton (1979) focused on a sample of 146 addicted females from therapeutic community and methadone treatment centers in Detroit, Los Angeles, and Miami. Among other findings, Colton noted:

Addicted women as compared to [nonaddicted women] appear to be lower in self-esteem, higher in reported symptoms of depression and anxiety, more open to relationships (less counter-dependent), lower in masculinity and femininity, and higher in assertiveness. (p. 31)

Yet, relative to addicted men, addicted women in Colton's sample had a number of positive qualities. According to Colton,

Women are more interested in and open to interpersonal relationships than the men, and also more responsive to the feelings of others. As evidenced by their scores on the Sex-Role Values Scale, these women have been taught to downplay and devalue these aspects of themselves. This is probably due both to the attitudes of the men they come into contact with, and to the realities of surviving in the drug culture. Treatment programs could foster those strengths and emphasize their value while at the same time training women in the skills which they may lack. (pp. 31-32)

These findings, together with reports of parenting awareness among addicted mothers, lay the foundation for positively oriented treatment programs that build on clients' strengths.

TREATMENT MODELS

The literature on effective treatment programs for addicted mothers is not large. For example, a compendium of research studies on drug abuse issues among women edited by Glynn, Pearson, and Sayers (1983) suggests the preponderance of descriptive studies on the topic. The volume also reveals the dearth of viable treatment recommendations and the absence of innovative treatment programs that have been subjected to rigorous and controlled empirical outcome research. Of 136 entries in the volume edited by Glynn et al., 48 reports are descriptive studies and 24 reports recommend — but do not describe — treatment approaches. No reports in the volume detail controlled outcome studies of treatment approaches with addicted women. What is more, preventive intervention as a treatment alternative received but a single mention in the Glynn et al. compendium. And that entry is in the context of directions for future and needed research.

As also recounted in the Glynn et al. (1983) edited volume, vast differences separate the treatment needs of ethnic-racial minority culture and majority culture women. Others too note these differences (cf. Wright, Gonzalez, & Multine, 1979). Investigators, clinicians, and program planners must therefore examine and seek to understand ethnic-racial differences when attempting to develop responsive treatments for the drug abuse and mental illness problems of minority and majority culture women.

Mindful of these caveats, professionals charged with the development of programs and services for dually impaired mothers can beneficially adapt treatment strategies from related areas of mental health and substance abuse treatment. In the following paragraphs, we review those treatment strategy possibilities.

Social Supports

At the conclusion of her descriptive study of addicted women, Tucker (1979) suggested that innovative treatments should seek to strengthen and build social supports available to the target clients. In particular, Tucker recommended:

> When a woman has an adequate support structure, it should be utilized to her advantage. For example, [therapists should] help other family members understand the treatment process and how they might help; [therapists should] get more couples into treatment (since addicted women are likely to be associated with addicted partners) and into mutually supportive roles. When a woman's support structure appears to be inadequate, [therapists should] develop workable intervention techniques and provide reasonable alternatives. (p. 73)

Illustrative of interventions and supports to increase and enhance this latter type of support structure are homemaker services, cooperative baby sitting efforts, and strategies that enable women to help each other with daily living tasks.

Along with efforts to nurture and sustain positive social supports among addicted women in treatment, therapeutic programs could seek to establish and reinforce patterns of positive child-management skills. For example, these efforts could profitably draw from early intervention programs for young, inexperienced mothers and their infants (Thompson, Cappleman, Conrad, & Jordan, 1982).

Alcohol Abuse Treatments
and Stress Management

Additional guidelines for innovative treatment programs for the target population of dually impaired mothers come from literatures related to group therapy formats and other treatments for clients with alcohol abuse problems. Stress management research provides another source of treatment guidelines. Regarding treatment services for alcohol abusing women, Vanicelli (1986) joins a number of investigators in recommending group formats. Group interventions, with roots in psychotherapy and in the fields of alcohol and drug abuse, offer obvious benefits of economy, vicarious learning, support, and opportunities for peer leadership.

In addition to these benefits, group milieus provide therapists and clinical researchers with data on the processes and interactions of treatment. Process data, encompassing such factors as meeting attendance, interactional styles, and natural support networks are a source of feedback and treatment guidance for professional staff who attend or observe group sessions. In the residential setting, group interaction data can thereby inform and direct other treatment programs and services for substance abusing and mentally ill mothers.

Additional techniques that hold promise for substance abusing, mentally ill mothers, also adapted from alcoholism treatment approaches with women, were put forth by McCrady (1984). These techniques include:

> The use of self-monitoring for assessing the relationship between drinking and other problem areas [and] The use of alternate skills training in treatment, the development of alternative support of reinforcement systems. (p. 447)

Another related and emerging body of literature comes from recent work on psychosocial stress.

Clinicians and investigators who work with and study issues of psychosocial stress among women report successful coping skills training through such techniques as relaxation, exercise, massage, and cognitive restructuring strategies (cf. Morse & First, 1982). Other intervention strategies that may lend themselves to the treatment of dually impaired mothers are skills training procedures.

Skills Interventions

Recent years have seen much research on skills interventions for treating and preventing substance abuse, primarily among young people (cf. Botvin & Wills, 1985; Schinke & Gilchrist, 1985). Skills interventions — so called because of their emphasis on learning theory-derived interpersonal skills, cognitive-behavioral skills, or life skills — teach people to avoid drug and alcohol abuse through a repertoire of strategies. Encompassing problem solving, personal coping, and interpersonal communication, skills interventions help people prevent substance abuse by managing themselves, others, and high-risk situations.

Increasingly, skills interventions also emphasize health and life-style promoting strategies. Through health promoting strategies, clients learn to advance their lives educationally, vocationally, and socially while they avoid drug and alcohol abuse. Illustrative are cognitive-behavioral interventions. As developed and tested in the past, cognitive-behavioral interventions help clients apply problem solving, self-appraisal, nonverbal and verbal communication, and social skills to avoid drug and alcohol abuse and to promote their lives in positive ways.

To date, skills interventions to prevent substance abuse have been mostly tested with children and adolescents. This limited testing is partly a function of the school systems that have been field research settings for the bulk of skills intervention studies. To a lesser through not insignificant extent, the absence of skills interventions for adult substance abusers is also explained by a paucity of research aimed expressly at these clients, particularly research with ethnic-racial minority populations from disadvantaged, inner-city communities.

The many published studies of skills interventions with non-minority, children and adolescents and the paucity of such intervention research with adult and disadvantaged populations are not unrelated. The demands of longitudinal studies along with the realities of public school enrollments create a climate that fosters intervention studies with stable, compliant, homogenous student populations.

Still, because of their potential to effect positive behavior change among mothers with a history of substance abuse and mental illness, skills interventions warrant consideration. Indeed, skills-based strategies have enjoyed wide use and are currently employed in many adult treatment programs for substance abusers. Though not as well published, treatment efforts and therapeutic programs for adults that are based on skills training models seek to enhance clients' home care competencies, educational and vocational advancement, and computer literacy, to name the common uses of these intervention approaches.

The conceptual rationale for skills intervention draws heavily from social learning theory (Bandura, 1969). Writing from a social learning theory perspective, Schinke and Gilchrist (1984) said, "behavior is the product of a transaction between the internal environment (attentional processes, thoughts, beliefs) and the external environment (events, sensory observations)" (p. 9). Thus, behavior is developed and sustained through this interaction. Again, according to Schinke and Gilchrist (1984), "People tend to behave in ways they believe will bring reinforcement and avoid punishment. Beliefs about what is reinforcing and what is punishing are shaped by the social environment" (p. 9).

Schinke and Gilchrist (1984) further laid out the essential theoretical argument for social learning based skills training to change human behavior:

> According to social learning theory, success in performing some task leads to feelings of mastery, efficacy, self-validation, and self-reinforcement. Recognition of personal efficacy increases willingness to repeat the same behavior again. Repeated practice generates higher levels of skill and more self-confidence in a spiraling learning cycle. . . . Such learning cycles can be deliberately accelerated. The life skills training approach . . . rests on this foundation from social learning

theory. The skills training approach assumes that problem behavior . . . is the result of faulty or incomplete learning, not
psychological illness. (p. 9)

Through five intervention elements—structure, information,
problem solving, self-instruction, coping, and communications—
skills interventions aim to redress or correct problems of incomplete
or faulty learning. The following sections describe these elements
relative to their potential application with mothers who have histories of drug use and mental illness.

Structure, for present purposes, refers to the manner in which
substance abusing and mentally ill mothers regard, employ, and
alter their available time. Time and how it is viewed and valued are
necessarily subjective concepts. Among substance involved clients
and clients with mental disorders, time may have less defined parameters than among clients who are less functionally impaired.
Thus, the first task of skills based interventions with dually diagnosed mothers is to help clients order and control their time.

These tasks can occur through prearranged structures for clients'
days and weeks in treatment. Certain limits and constraints may be
introduced to further instill in clients a renewed sense of time. Over
a period of treatment—whether on an out-patient basis or within a
residential setting—clients may then begin to alter not only their use
of time, but also their perceptions of time.

Information, accurate, timely, and relevant, is crucial for clients
to understand their problems and to reach and execute effective decisions on how to solve those problems. Respective to the target
client population of dually impaired mothers, information should
span the areas of substance abuse, mental illness, and parenthood.
For example, clients deserve to know the latest facts on short- and
long-term effects of substance use for themselves and for their children, on the nature, treatment, and prognosis of their mental disorder, and on efficacious and proven child management strategies.

Depending on the treatment context, information can be transmitted orally, through posters and cartoons, by audio-visual electronic
media, or via a combination of these methods. Information is used
best when it is culture- and age-relevant and, naturally, when it is
expressed in the language of target clients.

Problem solving, through a stepwise process, could allow clients to review chronic and difficult situations in their lives and then to brainstorm potential solutions. In turn, solutions can be ranked by individual clients or within small groups of clients according to their attractiveness and feasibility. Through such a review of the costs and likely consequences of particular solutions, clients can arrive at an optimal course of action. The completion of problem solving flow charts is often incorporated into homework assignments for purposes of practice.

Relative to the difficulties facing dually impaired mothers in the present target population, problem-solving techniques are increasingly applied to child-management and child abuse and neglect issues (Dawson, Armas, McGrath, & Kelly, 1986; Kirkham, Schinke, Schilling, Meltzer, & Norelius, 1986).

Self-instruction defines an intervention element that clients can employ as a portable means to alter their behavior in high-risk situations involving substance use, child management issues, or a host of interactional and intrapersonal areas. By rehearsing events and thoughts that accompany typical and everyday routines, clients can prepare for problem situations before they occur. Inner dialogues for self-instruction can follow semistructured formats.

Illustrative is the format using the acronym SODAS that we have applied in past researches with adolescents at risk for substance abuse (Schinke & Gilchrist, 1985; Schinke, Orlandi, Botvin, Gilchrist, Trimble, & Locklear, 1988). The letters in this acronym stand for Stop, Options, Decide, Act, and Self Praise and represent an example of a self-instructional teaching aid.

Coping as a skills based intervention strategy, recognizes the role of substance use as a means to manage or reduce stress. To support the relevance of coping as a skills intervention strategy are data that show the use of drugs and other substances as a maladaptive stress coping mechanism (Dembo, Blount, Schmeidler, & Burgos, 1986). Coping skills enable clients to anticipate and prepare for stressful and unpleasant situations, difficult obstacles, and challenges.

Regardless of their target, coping skills can include covert and overt mechanisms. Covert coping consists of cognitive processes that will aid clients to successfully confront potentially high risk situations. Overt coping occurs through behaviorally oriented mechanisms, including tangible self-rewards once clients success-fully overcome problem situations or circumstances.

Communication skills, via appropriate and effective nonverbal and verbal behaviors, are associated with social competence and interpersonal assertiveness. Hence, communications skills are inte-gral to life skills training for mothers at risk for substance abuse and mental health problems. To train clients in communication skills, live and symbolic modeling are first employed. Next, clients prac-tice what they learn through role plays. Professional and peer rein-forcement are employed for feedback purposes, with videotaping often used as an additional feedback mechanism.

PROGRAM PLANNING FOR INNOVATIVE SERVICES

Concurrent with the design of enriched treatment services adapted to the needs of women who have mental health and sub-stance abuse problems, program planners must guard against defin-ing women as pathological. Guarding against inadvertently devel-oping interventions that either foster more pathology or that do not lead toward competence is crucial. Program planners who look for clients' strengths to build an intervention and treatment plan will be apt to discover innovative modes of service delivery.

As an example, one team of investigators advocated the use of community-based, small group, and peer-led intervention models for mental health service delivery with women (Rickel, Forsberg, Gerrard, & Iscoe, 1984). As for the professional's role in such ser-vice delivery, Rickel et al. observed:

> The mental health professional's role in this environment is altered as well. Instead of being the on-line deliverer of ser-vice, the trained professional becomes consultant, educator, and trainer. (p. 305)

These facilitative roles of mental health professionals often have parallels in therapeutic communities, residential treatment pro-grams, and half-way house environments.

In fact, some models for community based treatment of mothers and children exist (cf. Cuskey, Richardson, & Berger, 1979; Dalton

& West, 1979; Lief, 1981). For instance, Odyssey House in New York City provides residential services for substance abusing mothers and for their children. Another such program in Norristown, Pennsylvania, that existed in 1982 was called Family House.

This residential treatment setting had a number of therapeutic elements. The range and depth of elements suggest the complexities of a comprehensive approach to treating mothers and children together in the presence of substance abuse problems or a recent history of drug use (Pearlman, West, & Dalton, 1982).

After an intake and initial assessment process, Family House residents undergo a treatment program that includes parenting seminars, sexuality seminars, health care training, and child care instruction. Reentry into the community is additionally accompanied by such services for mothers as financial counseling, child care arrangements, and community resources contacts.

The challenges and rewards of Family House and of potentially other community-based services for substance abusing mothers and their children is nicely summarized by Pearlman et al. (1982):

> Staff members in such programs . . . must be flexible, sensitive, and capable of independent action yet able to work as a team, comfortable in multiple roles, with knowledge of the treatment needs not only of drug dependent women but also of children . . . Because intense involvement with families is required, most staff cannot work with more than two or three families at a time. . . . The rewards of working in such a program are many and varied. In the daily contacts with mother and child, small successes are readily noticed. As mothers and children become more able to enjoy and appreciate each other, not only are the lives of the women enriched, but the prospects for their children's future are enhanced. (p. 558)

Clearly, Family House and similar environments offer promise as vehicles for delivery multiple mental health, substance abuse treatment, and child rearing services. This promise, however, is tempered by the costs of residential, home-based services in staff time and resources.

RESEARCH STRATEGIES

Clinical and programmatic efforts in the development and implementation of new services for mothers who have a history of substance abuse and mental illness, as with any nascent field of behavioral and social sciences, must inevitably begin without a preexisting knowledge base. The absence of empirical knowledge in this area, however, should be quickly remediated as programs and treatment strategies emerge. Those programs and strategies in turn will wisely include a careful evaluation system.

Evaluation methods for innovative clinical programs must focus equally on process and outcome assessments. Process assessments measure intervention delivery by documenting such implementation parameters as therapist behaviors, client reactions, and logistical and procedural details. Outcome assessments measure the effects of intervention respective to client knowledge, attitudes, and behaviors. Once programs are underway, investigators can perform impact assessments. These assessments measure not only additional client variables, but also such parameters as changes in the family members, significant others, workplaces, and communities that surround clients and treatment programs.

Evaluation must concentrate as much on qualitative and case-report differences in outcomes as on quantitative and statistically meaningful differences. As summarized by Wallston and Grady (1985) relative to research on women and gender, statistics and inference must be carefully balanced in studies of new and less well known phenomena:

> The study of women and gender has raised issues relating to the nature of statistics and their utilization. The consistent theme is the relation among the statistics we use, the questions we ask, and the inferences we draw. To the extent that statistics restrict our questions, we must work on the development of alternative statistics and the more adequate use of available statistics. (p. 26)

Far from representing the final step in innovative service program delivery with dually diagnosed substance abusing and mentally ill mothers, evaluation should begin the process of iterative program refinement and improvement as each piece of evaluation data enhances our understanding of what works and of what makes a difference in intervention programming.

CONCLUSION AND FUTURE DIRECTIONS

In this paper, we have initiated a discussion of the special challenges that face mothers who use drugs and who have mental problems. We have also reviewed potential intervention strategies for human services professionals interested in helping these mothers. Doubtless, the complexities of any dually diagnosed client population do not lend themselves to facile solutions. Yet, the difficulties of women who are at once mothers, past or current substance users, and mentally or emotionally handicapped appear particularly nettlesome for treatment and program planning.

Our suggestions for beginning such treatment and program planning, therefore, are necessarily tentative and untested. Until more is known about members of the target client population and until additional resources are forthcoming to help these clients, definitive guidelines for research, program planning, and service delivery are impossible. Even so, the pressing needs of dual diagnosed, substance abusing and mentally ill mothers and their children demand action. In the absence of empirical data on exact program needs of these clients and children, innovative programs are timely and appropriate.

While beginning to develop programs responsive to the target population of mothers and children, we have noted the potential benefits of comprehensive residential treatment programs and skills based interventions. Specifically, we have drawn from extant literature on problems related to the needs of substance abusing and mentally ill mothers to identify promising intervention strategies. These literatures concern the fields of mental health, substance abuse treatment, social supports, child abuse and neglect, home- and community-based treatment milieus, and skills oriented preventive intervention and early intervention approaches.

The future agenda for program planning, research, and treatment services delivery with mothers who have a history of substance abuse and mental illness is vast. To concurrently address several agenda items, new programs for the target clients must include careful evaluation components to document the processes, outcomes, and, eventually, the impact of innovative programs. Our nascent efforts at Project Return Foundation, in New York City, aimed at better serving the target population of mothers and their children, will follow such a multiple-track pattern.

Though still at a preliminary stage, Project Return Foundation's treatment program for dual diagnosed, substance abusing and mentally ill mothers and their children will express many of the concepts formulated in the foregoing sections. The residential program will have a skills-oriented program that recognizes the differential and jointly overlapping needs of mothers and children. Operationally, this recognition will take form in separate and distinct residential and treatment staffs for mothers and for children.

Everyday, mothers and children will have structured opportunities to interact verbally, nonverbally, and in purposeful play. By keeping the child care and maternal staffs separate, the Project Return Foundation program will avoid problems of staff over-identification, victim blaming, and possessiveness. We look forward to reporting in greater detail on the Project Return Foundation program for dual diagnosed mothers and children, once the residential treatment program is operational.

Warranting reiteration is that this paper has confined its coverage to the special needs and treatment considerations for dually diagnosed, substance abusing and mentally ill mothers. Due to this focus, we have narrowed our discussion to those issues most salient and least researched with members of the target population. Less definitive than suggestive, the paper has not reviewed the state-of-the-art of substance abuse treatment, residential treatment, or mental health treatment.

Given these caveats, perhaps the discussion and guidelines offered here will urge our colleagues and other like-minded clinical researchers to also pursue investigations and program development, testing, and refinement in this most-pressing area.

REFERENCES

Bandura, A. (1969). *Principles of behavior modification*. New York: Holt, Rinehart and Winston.

Bauman, P. & Dougherty, F. (1983). Drug addicted mothers parenting and their children's development. *International Journal of the Addictions, 88*, 291-302.

Billing, L. Eriksson, M., Larsson, G. & Zellerstrom, R. (1979). Occurrence of abuse and neglect of children born to amphetamine addicted mothers. *Child abuse and neglect, 3*.

Botvin, G. J., & Willis, T. A. (1985). Personal and social skills training: Cognitive-behavioral approaches to substance abuse prevention. In C. Bell, & R. Battjes (Eds.), *Prevention research: Deterring drug abuse among children and adolescents*. Washington, DC: NIDA, U.S. Government Printing Office.

Bowlby, J. (1966). *Maternal care and mental health*. New York: Schocken.

Colten, M. E. (1979). A descriptive and comparative analysis of self-perceptions and attitudes of heroin-addicted women. In *Addicted women: Family dynamics, self perceptions, and support systems* (NIDA Services Research Monograph Series). Rockville, MD: U.S. Department of Health, Education and Welfare.

Cuskey, W. R., Richardson, A. H., & Berger, L. H. (1979). *Specialized therapeutic community program for female addicts*. Washington, D.C.: U.S. Govt. Printing Office.

Dalton, J., & West, M. (1979). Mothers, children together: A new approach from Eagleville. *Focus on Alcohol and Drug Issues, 2*(3), 6-7.

Dawson, B., de Armas, A., Kelly, J. A., & McGrath, M. L. (1986). Cognitive problem-solving training to improve the child-care judgment of child neglectful parents. *Journal of Family Violence, 1*(3), 209-221.

Dembo, R., Blount, W. R., Schmeidler, J., & Burgos, W. (1986). Perceived environmental drug use risk and the correlates of early drug use or nonuse among inner-city youths: The motivated actor. *International Journal of the Addictions, 21*, 977-1000.

Eldred, C., Grier, V., & Berliner, N. (1974). Comprehensive treatment for heroin-addicted mothers. *Social Casework, 55*(8), 470-474.

Elliot, D. S., Huizinga, D. & Ageton, S. S. (1985). *Explaining delinquency and drug use*. Beverly Hills: Sage.

Fawzy, F., Coombs, R., & Gerber, B. (1983). Generational continuity in the use of substances: The impact of parental substance use on adolescent substance use. *Addictive Behaviors, 8*, 109-114.

Glynn, T. J., Pearson, H. W., & Sayers, M. (Eds.). (1983). *Research issues 31: Women and drugs*. Rockville, MD: National Institute on Drug Abuse.

Hawkins, J. D., Lishner, D. M., & Catalano, R. F. (1985). Childhood predictors and the prevention of adolescent substance abuse. In C. L. Jones & R. J. Battjes (Eds.), *Etiology of drug abuse: Implications for prevention*. Rockville, MD: NIDA.

Kirkham, M. A., Schinke, S. P., Schilling, R. F., Meltzer, N. J., & Norelius, K. L. (1986). Cognitive-behavioral skills, social supports, and child abuse potential among mothers of handicapped children. *Journal of Family Violence*, *1*(3), 235-245.

Lief, N. (1981). Parenting and child services for drug dependent women. In B. Reed, G. Beschner, & J. Mondanaro (Eds.), *Treatment services for drug dependent women* (Vol. 1). Washington, DC: U.S. Government Printing Office.

Loeber, R., & Tengs, T. (1986). The analysis of coercive chains between children, mothers, and siblings. *Journal of Family Violence*, *1*(1), 51-70.

McCrady, B. S. (1984). Women and alcoholism. In E. A. Blechman (Ed.), *Behavior modification with women*. New York: Guilford Press.

Mondanaro, J., Wdenoja, M., Densen-Gerber, J., Elahi, J., Mason, M. & Redmond, A. (1982). Sexuality and fear of intimacy as barriers to recovery for drug dependent women. In B. Reed, G. Beschner, & J. Mondanaro (Eds.), *Treatment services for drug dependent women* (Vol. 1). Washington, DC: U.S. Government Printing Office.

Morse, D. R., & Furst, M. L. (1982). *Women under stress*. New York: Van Nostrand Reinhold Company.

Needle, R. H., Glynn, T. J., & Needle, M. P. (1983). Drug abuse: Adolescent addictions and the family. In C. R. Figley & H. McCubbin (Eds.), *Stress and the Family: Coping with Catastrophe* (Vol. II). New York: Brunner/Mazel.

New York State Department of Substance Abuse Services (1981). *Survey of households of substance abusers*. New York: NY.

New York State Department of Substance Abuse Services (1983). *Statewide comprehensive five year plan*. New York, NY.

Pearlman, P., West, M., & Dalton, J. (1982). Mothers and children together: Parenting in a substance abuse program. In B. Reed, G. Beschner, & J. Mondanaro (Eds.), *Treatment services for drug dependent women* (Vol. 2). Washington, DC: U.S. Government Printing Office.

Rickel, A. U., Forsberg, L. K., Gerrard, M., & Iscoe, I. (1984). New directions from women: Moving beyond the 1980's. In A. U. Rickel, M. Gerrard, & I. Iscoe (Eds.), *Social and psychological problems of women: Prevention and crisis intervention*. Washington: Hemisphere.

Rosenbaum, M. (1979). Difficulties in taking care of business: Women addicts as mothers. *American Journal of Drug and Alcohol Abuse*, *6*(4), 431-446.

Rowe, C. (1981). *An outline of psychiatry*. Dubuque: Wm. C. Brown.

Schindler, F., & Arkowitz, H. (1986). The assessment of mother-child interactions in physically abusive and nonabusive families. *Journal of Family Violence*, *1*(3), 247-257.

Schinke, S. P., & Gilchrist, L. D. (1984). *Life skills counseling with adolescents*. Baltimore: University Park Press.

Schinke, S. P., & Gilchrist, L. D. (1985). Preventing substance abuse with children and adolescents. *Journal of Consulting and Clinical Psychology*, *53*, 596-602.

Schinke, S. P., Orlandi, M. A., Botvin, G. J., Gilchrist, L. D., Trimble, J. E. & Locklear, V. S. (1988). Preventing substance abuse among American Indian adolescents: A bicultural competence skills approach. *Journal of Counseling Psychology*, *35*, 87-90.

Semidei, J. (1983). At special risk: Phase 1 report. New York, NY: Office of Human Development Services.

Suffet, F., Bryce-Buchanan, C. & Brotman, R. (1981). Pregnant addicts in a comprehensive care program: Results of a follow-up survey. *American Journal of Orthopsychiatry*, *51*, 297-306.

Sutker, P. (1981). Drug dependent women. In B. Reed, G. Beschner, & J. Mondanaro (Eds.), *Treatment services for drug dependent women* (Vol. 1). Washington, DC: U.S. Government Printing Office.

Thompson, R. J., Cappleman, M. W., Conrad, H. H., & Jordan, W. B. (1982). Early intervention program for adolescent mothers and their infants. *Developmental and Behavioral Pediatrics*, *3*(1), 18-21.

Tucker, B. (1979). A descriptive and comparative analysis of the social support structure for heroin-addicted women. In *Addicted women: Family dynamics, self perceptions, and support systems* (NIDA Research Monograph series). Washington, DC: U.S. Government Printing Office.

Vannicelli, M. (1986). Treatment considerations. In *Women and alcohol: Health related issues* (Research Monograph 16). Rockville, MD: U.S. Department of Health and Human Services.

Wallston, B. S., & Grady, K. E. (1985). Integrating the feminist critique and the crisis in social psychology: Another look at research methods. In V. E. O'Leary, R. K. Unger, & B. S. Wallston (Eds.), *Women, gender and social psychology*. Hillsdale, NJ: Lawrence Erlbaum Associates.

Wellisch, D. & Steinberg, M. (1980). Parenting attitudes of addicted mothers. *International Journal of the Addictions*, *15*, 809-819.

Wright, I., Gonzalez, J., & Multine, T. (1979). Minority women: Their special problems. In R. Crow & G. McCarthy (Eds.), *Teenage women in the juvenile justice system*. Tucson, AZ: New Directions for Young Women.

Drug Use and Felony Crime: Biochemical Credibility and Unsettled Questions

Nathaniel J. Pallone

SUMMARY. Though there is widespread belief that drug abuse is related to felony crime, precise linkages have not yet been established, in some measure because prospective linkages have been studied not only through the variant methods of social and "hard" science, but also because the methods of biochemical laboratory assay developed to detect the presence of drugs in the physical system have become more technologically discerning. Representative studies from the social sciences, relying on the self-reports of convicted felons, and from the "hard" sciences, utilizing "more" and "less" sensitive methods of laboratory assay, yield data that propose, at the extremes, that one of every six *or* one of every two felonies is at the least "lubricated" by drug use or abuse. But there is insufficient evidence as yet to conclude to the *differential* effects of *specific* substances with known biochemical properties that produce particular biochemical effects on the acceleration of *particular* types of felony crime. In future inquiry to establish such precise links, biochemistry and neuropsychopharmacology will take the lead. Largely as a result of the introduction of wide-scale drug testing of worker populations, increased attention has been engendered among biomedical scientists about "bandwidth fidelity" issues in the detection of controlled dangerous substances. Adoption in several states of "pathological intoxication" laws endorsed by the American Psychiatric Association and the burgeoning of the "designer drug" industry combine to produce a forensic Wonderland.

Nathaniel J. Pallone, PhD, is University Distinguished Professor, Clinical Psychology & Criminal Justice, Rutgers University, New Brunswick, where he previously served as Dean and as Academic Vice President.

This article is based on a paper presented at the 35th International Congress on Alcoholism and Drug Dependence, Oslo, August 1988.

The United States is a nation apparently obsessed by the use and abuse of chemical substances. In a typical year, the aggregate total of arrests made *exclusively* for offenses related to sale and possession of "controlled dangerous substances" (opium, cocaine, marijuana, or synthetics) or to alcohol (driving under the influence, public drunkenness, other violations of liquor laws, such as sale to minors) is nearly double the aggregate total of arrests made in all jurisdictions for all *felony crimes combined* [cf. McGarrell & Flanagan, 1985, pp. 451-461]. Of all arrests (some 12,000,000) in all jurisdictions in the U.S. for all offenses (felony, misdemeanor), some 449,000 are made for violent felonies and some 1,930,000 for property felonies, while some 3,500,000 are made *exclusively* for alcohol offenses and some 662,000 *exclusively* for drug offenses *not* associated with those felony crimes enumerated in the U. S. Department of Justice's Index of Serious Crime (i.e., homicide, assault, rape, robbery, weapons possession, burglary, forgery or fraud, larceny).

Though arrests for specific drug offenses account for a discernible proportion of all U.S. arrest activity, is there evidence that the use of "controlled dangerous substances" contributes to the commission of other crimes, particularly of felonies? From Wolfgang's studies in the 1950's onward, a considerable body of research evidence, much of it summarized by Collins [1981] and Roizen [1981], appears to have established a consistent link between alcohol and violent crime. But, despite what is generally conceded to be an "epidemic" in the use of "controlled dangerous substances" within the past two decades and the consequent and widespread belief that drug use/abuse similarly represents a contributory factor in felony crime, reinforced by press accounts that focus only on the proportion of arrest activity related exclusively to drug offenses without simultaneous explanation that these arrests are *not* related to felony offenses [Graham, 1987], little systematic research effort has been undertaken to establish precise linkages. The determination of consistent linkages of stable magnitude is important at the theoretical level in the understanding of criminogenesis and, at the pragmatic level, both in the design of programs of rehabilitation or treatment in the jails and prisons and/or through pre-trial diversion programs and in the determination of criminal responsibility in individual cases by way of specification of aggravating or mitigating factors.

ENGINE, LUBRICANT, OR MOTIVE?

Conceptually, the use or abuse of psychoactive substances — whether "controlled" and "dangerous" or not, and whether obtained illegally or through medical prescription — might be associated with felony crime in several ways: .

- As *engine*, functioning so as to induce a person "under the influence" to commit a criminal act of which he/she might otherwise seem incapable. An otherwise peaceable male ingests a particularly strong dose of a mood-altering central nervous system stimulant (e.g., illegally-obtained LSD *or* medically-obtained amphetamine), for example, quickly develops the delusion that he possesses super-human strength and simultaneously finds himself intolerant of disagreement by others; a fistic conflict ensues, resulting in a charge of aggravated assault.
- As *lubricant*, functioning so as to facilitate what, at least *post-hoc*, appears to be a predisposition to criminal behavior. An otherwise well-controlled but sexually undiscriminating man in his mid-30's, for example, ingests a quantity of a central nervous system depressant (marijuana, barbiturates), and, while "under the influence," appears to "lose" the capacity to differentiate the ages of women younger than himself, and is charged with statutory rape.
- As *motive*, functioning as the goal to which criminal activity is directed. A person long habituated to heroin, for example, or to certain cough syrups for that matter, burglarizes a suburban house in order to obtain goods than can be sold to support his habit — with the crime committed typically while this offender is *not* "under the influence."

The *engine* and *lubricant* functions correspond to what McGlothlin [1985] has called the "direct pharmacological effects" of drug use, among which he catalogs "drug-induced disinhibition resulting in impulsive actions, crimes of negligence such as those result-ing from driver-impaired performance, and the occasionally re-ported use of drugs . . . as a means of fortifying [oneself] to engage in criminal activities," while the *motive* function corresponds to what he has called an "indirect pharmacological effect."

To establish precise links between drug use/abuse and felony crime, the research evidence should reveal *what* controlled danger-ous substances function as engine, lubricant, or motive in relation to *which* crimes. Self-report evidence from convicted offenders concerning whether they were or were not "under the influence" during criminal activity may be inadequate to illuminate precise linkages with biochemical credibility unless accompanied by bio-chemical verification; but biochemical evidence concerning whether arrestees were "under the influence" at the point of arrest, especially if not under "hot pursuit" circumstances, may be insuf-ficient to determine whether drug use/abuse functions *phenomeno-logically* either as engine or as lubricant for criminal behavior.

BIOCHEMICAL CREDIBILITY

For a variety of reasons, however, the current body of research data fails of such precision. A particularly troublesome lacuna in the literature is the absence of careful consideration of the typical *biochemically-determined neuropsychological sequelae* to the use and abuse of psychoactive substances of various sorts. Indeed, among current studies, McGlothlin's [1985] alone is attentive to biochemical issues in a meaningful way. As cataloged in a variety of standard sources on psychopharmacology [e.g., Hofmann & Hofmann, 1975; Schatzberg & Cole, 1986; Perry, 1987], each of the major classes of "abusable" drugs possesses specific biochem-ical properties which produce predictable neuropsychological se-quelae; these range from euphoria, aggressivity, and overwhelming impulsivity (as in the case of psychotomimetic central nervous sys-tem stimulants, such as cocaine and the amphetamines) to persistent passivity and withdrawal (as in the case of narcoleptic central ner-vous system sedatives and depressants).

Is it reasonable to believe that substances with variant biochem-ical properties contribute equally and uniformly to criminal activity across the spectrum of types of felony crime, regardless of the character of each type of crime? Or is it more reasonable to suppose that "abusable" substances may be *differentially* related to the emission of criminal behavior of one sort, but not of other sorts — i.e, that the use/abuse of drugs with particular biochemical properties which produce predictable, but very particular, neuropsychological effects accelerates or contributes to particular types of criminal activity, but not necessarily to other types?

Absent contrary evidence, it is *biochemically credible* to suppose that the use or abuse of *central nervous system stimulants* and perhaps of hallucinogens accelerates *crimes of violence and personal victimization*. Among the property crimes, it seems likely that *burglary* alone might be accelerated by stimulants. Conversely, it is likely that the *central nervous system depressants retard violent behavior* of all sorts. These speculations, however, do not necessarily point to drug use or abuse as the primary *engine* for crime; instead, drug use might more convincingly be regarded as a *lubricant* which potentiates other pre-disposing factors, both intra- and extra-personal. And almost certainly it is the *"profit crimes"* of burglary and robbery that are implicated when the acquisition of abusable substances functions as *motive*. In McGlothlin's [1985, pp. 154-155] formulation:

> . . . there is some evidence that drug use contributes to crime directly by potentiating impulsive and violent behavior; however, the overall significance of this contribution is certainly small . . . barbiturates have been found to potentiate assaultiveness . . . amphetamines and cocaine in high doses can produce paranoid reactions resulting in violence, although there are relatively few such accounts in the literature . . . Marijuana and the stronger hallucinogens are also capable of producing psychotic reactions, and there are occasional references to violent behavior during these episodes [but] marijuana typically decreases both expressed and experienced hostility . . . there is growing evidence that the pseudo-hallucinogen, phencyclidine, has a fairly high potential for producing combative and violent behavior . . . Opiates produce a reliable sedating reaction without the increased emotional lability and aggressive-

ness accompanying alcohol and barbiturate use. Thus, the pharmacological properties of opiates would be expected to decrease rather than potentiate criminal behavior, and this is generally consistent with the available evidence . . . Finally, and perhaps this is the issue of major concern, there is the question of income-generating crime among individuals with expensive drug habits [and] commission of acquisitive crimes during a period of withdrawal.

CONFLICTING DATA FROM VARIANT METHODS OF INQUIRY

Earlier studies of the relationship between drug use/abuse and felony crime prototypically relied on data from self-reports, often of the offender but sometimes of the victim, as the standard index of criminogenic drug use or abuse, with but few inquiries relying on independent observations and yet fewer based on laboratory assessments of whether drugs (licit or illicit) could be detected in the physical system of an accused (or witnessed) offender. Independent observations (most often, by arresting police officers, or, far less frequently, by a knowledgeable witness) varied, but essentially only marginally, from self-reports of victim or offender. Current studies of the relationship between drug use/abuse and felony crime can be categorized by method of inquiry into those which utilize *self-report* data and those which employ *laboratory assay methods*. Among the self-report studies, there is a further distinction between those investigations which inquire into the *drug use/abuse habits of known offenders* and those which inquire into the *criminal behavior patterns of known drug users*. Among the laboratory assay studies, there is also a further distinction, predicated on the *"sensitivity" of the specific methodology* used to detect metabolites which biochemically succeed the ingestion of "controlled dangerous substances," typically among samples of arrestees; and then, given the relative infrequency of instant apprehension, often long after the criminal event.

Moreover, in virtually each report, it is necessary to regroup the reported data so as to eliminate those cases in which the offenses of record are related exclusively to drugs. With variant social science and biochemical research methodologies employed, and, frankly, given the tendency of social scientists to misconstrue data from the "hard" sciences, that the current body of evidence fails to yield firm conclusions concerning precise linkages between drug use/abuse and felony crime may not be surprising.

McGlothlin's Study of Known Drug Abusers

A number of investigations, of which McGlothlin's [1985] is a prime exemplar, have analyzed data on criminal activity among relatively small samples of known drug abusers, principally those who have applied for treatment in drug rehabilitation facilities operated by mental health authorities.

McGlothlin's sample consisted of some 581 self-identified male narcotics addicts (mean age = 25; no racial data supplied) admitted to a treatment program in California who were followed over a ten year period after admission through collection of police arrest records as well as interviews. Data concerning arrests for drug and other offenses, extent of drug dealing activity, employment, number of crimes self-reported annually, the number of man-days per year during which each subject self-reported as engaged in criminal activity, and a variety of other variables were arrayed in several ways. Of the several arrays, the most pertinent is that which contrasts subjects who used narcotics on a daily basis with those who used narcotics on other than a daily basis. In this contrast, the daily users ("addicts") were arrested significantly more frequently each year for *felony property offenses* and for *drug offenses*, but not for violent felonies; more frequently self-reported as engaged in drug dealing (58% vs. 16%); and self-reported a significantly higher number of *property* crimes per year (47 vs. 17), a higher level of income from crime ($9100 vs. $1700), and a significantly smaller proportion of man-days per year during which they were *not* engaged in criminal activity (53% vs. 83%).

Considering his own data and data from some 45 other studies that investigated the criminal behavior of *known* drug abusers over long periods of time, McGlothlin [1985, pp. 166-167] reached what he called "unequivocal conclusions" that "during periods of addiction, individuals are more likely to be arrested . . . to commit more crime, and to acquire more money from property crimes." Since the crimes committed by these known-addict subjects are predominantly property crimes (with the crimes of violence observed virtually invariably themselves associated with "drug deals gone sour"), McGlothlin's results seem to argue that, for abusers of one class of controlled dangerous substance, drug use functions primarily as *motive*.

U.S. Bureau of the Census Surveys of Jail and Prison Inmates

The most ambitious of the self-report studies of the drug use habits of accused and/or convicted offenders have been the demographic surveys of the jails and prisons conducted by the U.S. Bureau of the Census for the Department of Justice, based on interviews with inmates conducted according to standard schedules by trained Census interviewers. In one such study [Bureau of Justice Statistics, 1980], self-reports were obtained from some 91,411 jail inmates (94% male; 56.9% white) who had been *convicted* of felonies (29.5%) and awaiting incarceration in a state prison *or* of misdemeanors of various sorts (70.5%) and serving their sentences in these county jails. According to their self-reports, some 22% of the subjects in this largely misdemeanant pool were, at the time of the instant offense "under the influence of drugs." Marijuana led the list, with 7% of the subjects so stipulating, with heroin stipulated by 4%; 6% had used a combination of drugs (perhaps with antagonistic biochemical properties and neuropsychological sequelae) and 5% had used "other" drugs. While there is no indication that, upon admission to a jail facility, these self-reported drug abusers were actively toxic, the mildest implication to be drawn in respect of program design would point in the direction of multi-targeted drug education and rehabilitation, while the implication to be drawn in respect of criminogenesis would argue in the direction of a contributing or accelerating factor in criminal behavior — but without inflection in respect of type of crime.

The largely misdemeanant sample whose self-reports were just recited present a spectrum of criminal activity that, 70% of the time, is limited to minor crime and/or "public order" offenses, including violations of alcohol or drug laws or to related matters, such as driving under the influence. In the Census survey of *convicted offenders* published most recently [McGarrell & Flanagan, 1985, pp. 658-659; *Bulletin NCJ-875752*, 1983, p. 3], 274,564 convicted felons (96% male; 49.6% white) were interviewed.

When data are re-arrayed by major category, it is found that some *30%* of the incarcerated felons *convicted of violent crimes* and some *35%* of those *convicted of property crimes* self-reported as "under the influence" at the time of the instant offense. When data are re-arrayed according to sub-categories, the self-reported "positive" rate is 21% among prisoners convicted of criminal homicide, 27% among those convicted of assault, 22% among those convicted of rape, 38% among those convicted of robbery, 34% among those convicted of "other" violent crimes, 40% among those convicted of burglary, 25% among those convicted of forgery or fraud, 30% among those convicted of larceny, and 30% among those convicted of "other" property crimes.

The clearest implications from this massive study tend toward program design in prison facilities, since on the order of a third of all convicted felons identify themselves as "under the influence" at the time of the instant offense and could be expected to benefit from drug rehabilitation programming. Similarly, but not so strongly since type of crime is not inflected by type of drug used or abused, a modest link between substance abuse and criminogenesis is suggested in *each* of the major categories of felonious crime.

"Less Sensitive" Laboratory Assay: TLC Methodology

Thin-layer chromatography was utilized in a study by Creative SocioMedics Corporation [Richardson, Morein & Phin, 1978, Tables 13-47] which analyzed the urine specimens of 1816 *arrestees* (90.7% male; 49.2% white; 85.3% of all those arrested for all misdemeanors or felonies) in four "representative" U.S. counties (Dade, in Florida; Erie, in New York; King, in Washington; Maricopa, in Arizona) over a two-month period for the presence of a variety of "controlled dangerous substances" (amphetamine, ampitriptyline, barbiturate, cocaine, codeine, diphenhydramine, hydrox-

yzine, hydromorphine, meperidine, methadone, morphine, penta-
zocine, phenmetrazine, phenothiazine, propoxyphene, trimethoben-
zamide). Specimens were collected at point of admission to county
jail, immediately after arrest, whether under "hot pursuit" or other
circumstances, and were analyzed through thin-layer chromatography (TLC). When data for arrestees for suspected felony offenses
are re-arrayed by major categories, the "positive" rates found in
laboratory analyses yield remarkable contrasts with the Census self-
report data among convicted felons just reviewed. The positive
rates found by TLC laboratory assay among arrestees for felony
crime generally are lower than the self-report rates by at least 50%,
with *14% of violent crime arrestees* and *17% of property crime
arrestees* found drug positive.

When data are re-arrayed according to sub-categories, the labora-
tory-determined "positive" rate is 45% among arrestees for homicide, 12% among arrestees for assault, 17% among arrestees for
rape, 18% among arrestees for robbery, 8% among arrestees for
"other" violent crimes, 14% among arrestees for burglary, 16%
among arrestees for forgery or fraud, 19% among arrestees for larceny, and 18% among those convicted of "other" property crimes.

"More Sensitive" Laboratory Assay:
EMIT Methodology

The TLC methodology used in the CJDASS study is a "less sensitive" method of laboratory assay. In contrast, Hofmann & Hofmann [1975, p. 261] estimate that immunochemical methods of detection are "perhaps 1000 times more sensitive" to certain drugs
than TLC.

The NADRI/Manhattan Study: Such methods were utilized in
studies of arrestees in New York County, New York (Manhattan)
by Narcotic and Drug Research, Inc. [Wish, Brady & Cuadrado,
1986, Tables 1, 3]. Urine specimens for 5571 arrestees (97% male;
84% of all those arrested for felony or misdemeanor during a seven-
month period; no racial data indicated) for the presence of cocaine,
methadone, morphine, and phencyclidine (PCP) through "enzyme
multiplied immune urine tests" (EMIT), a laboratory methodology
that is described as "more sensitive for identifying recent drug use"

than TLC, such that "Estimates of drug use based on TLC [are] one half to two thirds lower than the estimates from EMIT tests" [Hofmann & Hofmann, 1975, p. 231].

Specimens were collected in Manhattan Central Booking before subjects were sent to court for arraignment. When data for arrestees for suspected felony offenses (64% of all arrestees) are re-arrayed by major category of offense charged, the "positive" rates found by EMIT laboratory analysis are remarkably high; *53% among violent crime arrestees*, exceeding the rate in the Census study by a factor of 1.75 and that found in the CJDASS study by a factor of 3.75, and *57% among property crime arrestees*, exceeding the rate in the Census study by a factor of 1.62 and that in the CJDASS study by a factor of 3.35.

When data are re-arrayed according to sub-categories, the laboratory-determined "positive" rate is 56% among arrestees for homicide, 37% among arrestees for assault, 41% among arrestees for rape, 54% among arrestees for robbery, 53% among arrestees for "other" violent crimes, 59% among arrestees for burglary, 48% among arrestees for forgery or fraud, 56% among arrestees for larceny, and 61% among those convicted of "other" property crimes.

The NADRI Cocaine Study: In a second study, and one which appears to beg biochemical credibility, the NADRI researchers [Wish, 1987] focussed on a single substance — cocaine. Under similar circumstances, urine specimens for 429 arrestees (71% of all those arrested for felony or misdemeanor during a three-month period; no race or gender data indicated) for the presence of cocaine, *either* through the "more sensitive" EMIT *or* through the "less sensitive" TLC assay. In this sample, only four felony charges are represented. When arrestees for these four suspected felony offenses (47% of all arrestees) are arrayed by type of offense charged, the "positive" rates found for cocaine by the "more sensitive" EMIT procedures *or* the "less sensitive" TLC methods are incredibly high, generally exceeding the already markedly higher rates found in the first NADRI study (which had tested for a variety of substances, using the "more sensitive" EMIT procedures) by nearly 50% on average: 53% among assault arrestees, 83% among robbery arrestees, 77% among burglary arrestees, 56% among larceny arrestees.

The Toborg/District of Columbia Study. EMIT laboratory meth-odology was also utilized in a study of arrestees in the District of Columbia by Toborg Associates [Toborg & Bellassai, I, 1987; Toborg & Bellasai, IV, 1987, Tables 2-5]. Urine specimens for 6160 arrestees (82% male; apparently an indeterminate proportion of all those arrested for felony or misdemeanor between June 1984 and January 1985; 83% black; 34% charged with misdemeanors only; 41% with prior convictions for either felony or misdemeanor) for the presence of amphetamines, cocaine, heroin, methadone, and phencyclidine (PCP). In the District, arrestees for misdemeanors may be released by precinct police authorities after booking, fol-lowing a telephone interview with a member of the Pretrial Services Agency; those not so released are held in a Superior Court lock-up facility. Specimens were collected in this facility by a Pretrial Ser-vices Agency technician and analyzed on-site before subjects were sent to court for arraignment.

When data for arrestees for suspected felony offenses (66% of all arrestees) are re-arrayed according to standard nomenclature by ma-jor category of offense charged (with some curious gaps noted, since no arrests were reported in this sample for homicide, rape, or forgery/fraud), the "positive" rates found by EMIT laboratory analysis tend to exceed those by self-report inquiry among con-victed felons and those found by TLC methodolgy in the Creative SocioMedics study but to be somewhat lower than those reported by NADRI, also utilizing EMIT assay: *41% among violent crime ar-restees*, exceeding the rate in the Census study by a factor of 1.36 and that found in the CJDASS study by a factor of 2.92, but lower than that found in the NADRI study by a factor of 0.23, and *45% among property crime arrestees*, exceeding the rate in the Census study by a factor of 1.28 and that in the CJDASS study by a factor of 2.64, but lower than that found in the NADRI study by a factor of 0.22.

When data are re-arrayed according to sub-categories, the labora-tory-determined "positive" rate is 33% among arrestees for as-sault, 53% among arrestees for robbery, 42% among arrestees for "other" violent crimes, 42% among arrestees for burglary, 47% among arrestees for larceny, and 45% among those convicted of "other" property crimes.

HOW DISCREPANT ARE THE DISCREPANCIES?

One may compare and contrast the discrepant "drug positive" rates observed in the large scale studies reviewed in a variety of ways. Figure 1 graphically depicts the drug positive rates found by self-report in the Census study among felons convicted of *violent* crimes, arrayed by sub-category, with those found by "more" and "less" sensitive methods of laboratory assay in the CJDASS, NADRI, and Toborg studies; Figure 2 replicates the contrast with respect to *property* crimes.

For the statistical purist, the magnitude of these discrepancies can be gauged by applying the Chi-square statistic to test the significance of differences between proportions of samples of very different sizes. Thus:

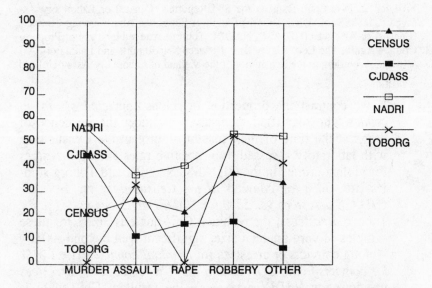

FIGURE 1. Discrepant Data on the Self-Reported (Census) or Laboratory Assayed (CJDASS, NADRI, Toborg) Extent of Substance Abuse among Convicts (Census) or Arrestees (CJDASS, NADRI, Toborg) Arrayed by Type of Violent Crime—The Levels Vary Both Between Self-Reports and Laboratory Assays and According to the Sensitivity of the Method of Laboratory Assay Utilized

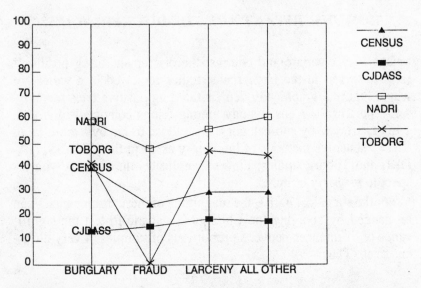

FIGURE 2. Discrepant Data on the Self-Reported (Census) or Laboratory As-sayed (CJDASS, NADRI, Toborg) Extent of Substance Abuse among Convicts (Census) or Arrestees (CJDASS, NADRI, Toborg) Arrayed by Type of Property Crime — Again, The Levels Vary Both Between Self-Reports and Laboratory As-says and According to the Sensitivity of the Method of Laboratory Assay Utilized

- If we contrast the proportion of felons *convicted of violent crimes* who identified themselves as under the influence of drugs at the time of their instant offense in the Census data with laboratory assessed drug positive rates among *arrestees* for violent crimes in the CJDASS, NADRI, and Toborg stud-ies (i.e, *30% for convicts in the Census data vs. 14% for CJDASS arrestees vs. 53% for NADRI arrestees vs. 41% for Toborg arrestees*), the resultant Chi-square is 36.51 for these samples of very unequal size, significant well beyond .001.
- Among convicts or arrestees for *criminal homicide* (i.e., *21% for convicts in the Census data vs. 45% for CJDASS arrestees vs. 56% for NADRI arrestees*), the resultant Chi-square is 26.55, significant beyond .01. No homicide arrestees are rep-resented in the Toborg data.
- Among convicts or arrestees for *rape* (i.e., *22% for convicts in*

the Census data vs. 17% for CJDASS arrestees vs. 42% for NADRI arrestees, with no rape arrestees represented in the Toborg sample), the resultant Chi-square is 28.52, significant beyond .001.

- Among convicts or arrestees for *other violent crimes* (i.e., *34% for convicts in the Census data vs. 8% for CJDASS arrestees vs. 53% for NADRI arrestees vs. 42% for Toborg arrestees*), the resultant Chi-square is 48.88, significant well beyond .001.
- For *property crime* convicts or arrestees as a group (i.e., *34% for convicts in the Census data vs. 17% for CJDASS arrestees vs. 57% for NADRI arrestees vs. 45% for Toborg arrestees*), the resultant Chi-square is 36.28, significant well beyond .001.
- Among convicts or arrestees for *burglary* (i.e., *40% for convicts in the Census data vs. 14% for CJDASS arrestees vs. 59% for NADRI arrestees vs. 42% for Toborg arrestees*), the resultant Chi-square is 43.60, significant beyond .001.
- Among convicts or arrestees for *forgery* (i.e., *25% for convicts in the Census data vs. 16% for CJDASS arrestees vs. 48% for NADRI arrestees, with no such arrestees in the Toborg data*), the resultant Chi-square is 26.10, significant beyond .001.
- Among convicts or arrestees for *larceny* (i.e., *30% for convicts in the Census data vs. 18% for CJDASS arrestees vs. 56% for NADRI arrestees vs. 47% for Toborg arrestees*), the resultant Chi-square is 29.49, significant beyond .001.
- Among convicts or arrestees for *other property crimes* (i.e., *30% for convicts in the Census data vs. 18% for CJDASS arrestees vs. 61% for NADRI arrestees vs. 45% for Toborg arrestees*), the resultant Chi-square is 43.97, significant beyond .001.

While the data from these studies fail to illuminate "precise linkages" between drug use/abuse and felony crime and similarly fail to reveal the relationship between use of mood-altering substances segregated even into gross categories (e.g., stimulant vs. depressant) and specific types of felony crime, one can draw few conclusions about whether such associations as are revealed portray drug use/abuse as engine, lubricant, or motive in a *biochemically credible* manner. Yet the data suggest a general and uninflected linkage of rather substantial proportions.

The orthogonal contrast is of the order of *1:6 vs. 1:2*; and that is quite a different matter than a diametric contrast like *1:6* (or 1:2) *vs. 0:1*. Moreover, given the advent of "designer drugs" resistant to detection by laboratory methods intended to detect controlled dangerous substances, these data may represent an underestimate of significant proportions.

However unsatisfactory the research picture may be from the perspective of the theory of criminogenesis, the implications, in the practical order, for management, security, and programming in correctional facilities and perhaps including provision for detoxification in county jails, are dramatic. If one opts to accept as a basis for planning the substantially lower rates reported by Creative SocioMedics, basing one's "bet" on the representativeness of the national sample, dismissing the more sensitive (and more expensive) EMIT technology as over-kill, and similarly dismissing the NADRI subjects as atypical because they represent Manhattan uniquely, one confronts the likelihood that on the order of one of every six felony arrestees has used a controlled dangerous substance recently enough that it is detectable through "less sensitive" laboratory assay. If one opts, on the other hand, for the rates reported in the NADRI study, basing one's "bet" on the greater sensitivity of the laboratory methodology employed and dismissing the atypicality of Manhattan arrestees in relation to the rest of the nation as carping noise, one confronts the likelihood that on the order of *one of every two* arrestees for felony crime has recently used such a substance, Similarly, despite the discrepancies between the self-reports of the *convicted and incarcerated* felons included in the Bureau of the Census enumerations and the laboratory assays, more and less sensitive, of felony *arrestees*, the implications for substance abuse education, rehabilitation, and prevention in the community and in correctional facilities seem clear enough.

"BANDWIDTH FIDELITY" IN THE ACCURACY OF DRUG TESTING

For the clinician concerned with determination of responsibility for felony crime, the situation is more muddled, particularly since the ingestion of mood-altering substances might constitute under some circumstances a "mitigating" and under other circumstances an "aggravating" factor.

So long as the matter of drug use remained an issue containerized largely within criminal justice circles, little serious attention was paid by biomedical scientists to questions concerning accuracy of the various laboratory assay methods of detection, the specific bio-chemical laboratory procedures used to extract samples of metabo-lites of various controlled dangerous substances from "parent" samples, sensitivity of each method to the metabolites of various "source" substances, rate of false positives (and false negatives), and "shelf life" of samples to be analyzed. Once the matter of large scale drug testing of worker populations became an issue in the workplace, and as "cottage industries" composed of testing labora-tories arose around the nation (coupled with other cottage industries which supply "alter ego" specimens to prospective examinees), however, that situation changed markedly. The journal *Seminars in Occupational Medicine*, for example, devoted its entire December 1986 issue to substance abuse in the workplace [Jackson, 1986]. Among that issue's contents, the reports of principal concern are those by Walsh & Gust on policy decisions on drug abuse, Schnoll & Lewis on drug screening protocols, and Bensinger on elasticity in interpretation of data. Similarly, Dwyer [1988], of the AFL-CIO's George Meany Center for Labor Studies, has recently complained that "tests conducted on real people in the work force falsely label one of out three (32.2%) positive for drugs."

The issues here appear essentially to be a specification of the "bandwidth fidelity" principle initially raised in another context by Cronbach & Glaser and recently resuscitated by Peterson [1987]: *the narrower the bandwidth, the greater the fidelity of measure-ment.*

The bandwidth fidelity argument in this context reduces to this sort of formulation: Since it is usually *not* a specific substance in the state of nature (that is, before being metabolized into a successor substance) that is discernible in post-ingestion analysis *but rather* the successor metabolite or metabolites, and since the successor substances are generally *not* uniquely related to a single source substance, it is almost certainly the case that laboratory analysis can accurately detect a specific "suspect" substance via its successor metabolite or metabolites with reasonable fidelity in a specific case *if the immediate ingestion history of the subject is known*. But it is also likely that *the fidelity of detection is reduced markedly when the number of suspect substances is increased* (as in broad-band laboratory assays for controlled dangerous substances of a variety of sorts, with quite different biochemical properties and metabolism routes) *and/or* when the immediate ingestion histories of large contingents of subjects are unknown — as indeed is the case in each of the laboratory assay studies reviewed here.

Without overly dwelling on the biochemistry involved, the flavor of these sets of issues can be gauged from a chapter on the forensic toxicology of cocaine by University of Utah toxicologists Finkle & McCloskey [1977, p. 169] in a National Institute on Drug Abuse Research Monograph on cocaine. After noting the prospect of "thermal degradation during analysis," Finkle & McCloskey observe of EMIT technology that it "has the advantage of . . . detection of the cocaine metabolite benzoylecgonine. However, for practical purposes it is insensitive to parent cocaine." Thus, the probability of a *false* negative *increases* when the sample to be analyzed has been extracted from subject shortly after ingestion and before metabolizing is completed; and the issue is engaged of what other substances, whether controlled and dangerous or not, in combination with other ingested materials are capable of producing the metabolite which EMIT technology is capable of detecting. That issue, in its turn, cannot be addressed without relatively detailed knowledge of the immediate ingestion history of the subject whose specimen is under analysis [cf. Finkle & McCloskey, 1977, p. 170].

Further, the matter is directly relevant to the burgeoning of the "designer drug" market in the U.S. If the decade between 1965 and 1975 can be characterized as the era of the narcoleptic and the hallucinogen in the U.S., that between 1975 and 1985 can be characterized as the era of the psychotomimetic, with a preference for cocaine and the amphetamines; and it seems likely that we have now entered the era of the synthetic "designer drugs." These are compounds developed in a burgeoning "cottage industry" which sets out quite consciously to avoid incorporating as an ingredient any substance which is labelled as "controlled" or "dangerous," thus producing substances which are putatively not illegal and highly resistant to detection by even the more sophisticated of the laboratory methodologies, not to say also less expensive at the point of sale and thus prospectively of wider market appeal.

The forensic implications are compelling. In a situation in which drug use may represent an aggravating factor, it is surely to the prosecutor's advantage to rely on wide bandwidth testing and to minimize the prospect of alternate origins for targeted metabolites, while it is surely to defense counsel's advantage to insist on bandwidth precision in assessing the presence of unique metabolites. In the reverse situation, where drug use represents a mitigating factor, defense counsel will prefer wide bandwidth assessment.

"PATHOLOGICAL INTOXICATION" AND CRIMINAL RESPONSIBILITY

In its 1982 statement on the insanity defense (in which, among many other things, it disavowed support for the "guilty but mentally ill" formulation incorporated into the laws of Michigan), the American Psychiatric Association [1984] essentially endorsed the position proposed by University of Virginia law professor R.J. Bonnie for a modification of the legal standard for insanity (and, by extension, diminished criminal responsibility) in the case of the "voluntary ingestion of alcohol or other psychoactive substances." Bonnie's formulation essentially amends the typical M'Naghten-inspired standard of the American Law Institute:

A person charged with a criminal offense should not be found guilty by reason of insanity if it is shown that as a result of mental disease or mental retardation he was unable to appreciate the wrongfulness of his conduct at the time of the offense. As used in this standard, the terms mental disease or mental retardation include only those severely abnormal mental conditions that grossly and demonstrably impair a person's perception or understanding of reality and that are not attributable primarily to the voluntary ingestion of alcohol or other psychoactive substances.

After publication of the Association's statement, a number of legislatures, including New Jersey's, adopted what are called "pathological intoxication" laws which directly incorporate either the Bonnie formulation or a close analogue thereto. In New Jersey, for example, the legislation contains a loophole to the effect that a defendant who has never ingested a particular substance before, and therefore cannot reasonably be expected to be able to have anticipated its effects upon him or her, may still claim involition or lack of knowledge in respect of a subsequent criminal act in his/her defense in a criminal proceeding.

If one considers the inconsistency implicit between the APA endorsement and the fact that not less than 15% of the total of 374 text pages in the newly issued revision to DSM-III is devoted to a cataloging of the several varieties of alcohol and substance abuse disorders, ranging from dependence to intoxication and delirium—with the latter two surely indicative of a state of mind that is, by the APA's own definitions, hardly congruent with unimpaired "perception or understanding of reality," let alone appreciation of the wrongfulness of one's conduct—one might suspect that Wonderland has arrived.

DETECTION OF "DESIGNER DRUGS"

If we add to the mix the burgeoning of cottage industries which manufacture "designer drugs" while deliberately avoiding incorporating as an ingredient any substance which is labelled as "controlled" or "dangerous," thus producing substances which are likely resistant to detection by wide bandwidth methodologies, the effects of which on the individual could be argued to be unknown precisely because of their novelty, the impression of a biochemical Wonderland is complete.

Dr. Robert Pandina of the Center for Alcohol Studies at Rutgers, for example, has identified the ingredients of a designer drug called "Love Boat," at least in what he calls the New Brunswick Formulary. These are formaldehyde, a disinfectant commonly available in hardware stores, Bull Durham cigarette tobacco, and rolling papers, commonly available at tobacconists, to say nothing of "head shops." In the construction of the substance, the tobacco is soaked in the formaldehyde, dried and rolled, then smoked. Once ingested by inhalation, the substance follows the route of aldehyde metabolism, emerging as aldehyde dehydrogenase or aldehyde reductase, enzymes which are implicated in the catabolism of norepinephrine and monoamine oxidase.

The phenomenological experience of the user will mimic that of the ingestion of cocaine, crack, amphetamine, or another psychotomimetic which interferes with MAO, though for a briefer period. Since the aldehyde metabolites are naturally-occurring following the ingestion of a variety of substances neither controlled nor dangerous, the ingestion of "Love Boat" is likely not detectable through laboratory analysis without a specific and immediate ingestion history to establish a "suspect" substance; and no laws concerning the acquisition of controlled dangerous substances appear to have been violated. Dr. Pandina and this writer were recently engaged, not incidentally, in a legal contest which focussed on whether a confirmed alcoholic who suffers from epileptiform disorder treated by an anticonvulsant should have foreseen that ingestion of this brand-new "designer drug" shortly after taking medically-prescribed Dilantin would lower the threshold level for convulsion, induce seizure yielding to delirium, and produce a hallucinatory state in which he identified his father as Satan. In what appears to have been the first successful challenge to the state's pathological intoxication laws, the jury decided that the novelty of the substance indeed precluded foreknowledge sufficient to exculpate the defendant from willful wrong-doing.

CONCLUSION

If this paper has been faithful to the present state of knowledge in the field, it has raised many questions and answered but few. It has been the sense of this paper that:

Precise links between drug use and felony crime remain conceptually indeterminate, though the evidence of a "general linkage" is strong. Though there is widespread belief that drug use/abuse is related to felony crime, the precise linkage has not yet been established, in some measure because such linkages have been studied not only through the variant methods of social and "hard" science, but also because the methods of laboratory assay developed in biochemistry to detect the presence of drugs in the physical system have become more technologically discerning. Relevant data from representative studies from the social sciences, relying on self-reports of convicted felons, and from the "hard" sciences, utilizing "more" and "less" sensitive methods of laboratory assay, propose, at the extremes, a general linkage such that one of every six *or* one of every two felonies is "lubricated" by drug use or abuse. A nascent major complication has been the burgeoning of the "designer drug" industry, producing substances resistant even to sophisticated laboratory detection, so that current data may well represent underestimates of the extent to which psychoactive substances are related to criminal behavior.

Varying "drug positive" rates may reflect divergent patterns of criminal disposition in certain jurisdictions as well as variant methods of inquiry. Since one expects to place greater credence in the data of "hard science," one might expect that laboratory assay studies would yield drug-positive rates that are discrepant with self-report data — but essentially in the same direction, whether positive *or* negative. But laboratory assay studies yield rates that are positively discrepant on the one hand and negatively discrepant on the other. Such diametric discrepancies might be attributed to the "more" and "less" sensitive methods of assay employed, recognizing the "bandwidth fidelity" issue in detecting successor metabolites to suspect substances.

But one might also look to systematic differences in various jurisdictions relating to arrest and to the progression from arrest to conviction and incarceration; and here jurisdictional particularities may well have a profound role. Given markedly low rates of indictment and conviction following arrest, is there any particularly sound reason to believe that more than a minor portion of the arrestees represented in these samples will later be incarcerated? What proportion of actively-toxic, readily-identifiable felony arrestees might reasonably be expected to find their way into a TASC substance abuse program, or another pre-trial intervention alternative? In what proportion of the cases might the abuse of drugs itself constitute the grounds for a "diminished responsibility" pleading that results in placement on probation, especially in the case of a first, non-violent felony offense? Some combination of such factors might well reconcile even the wide discrepancies observed both between self-report data and laboratory data and between data produced by variant methods of laboratory analysis.

Self-reports may be the only viable route to determining whether drug use functioned biochemically as "engine" or "lubricant" in criminal behavior and that situation may be even further exacerbated by the availability of "designer drugs" relatively less detectable by even sophisticated laboratory assay. To be useful to a theory of the genesis of crime, research on drug use/abuse among offenders should first establish *whether* substance use functions as *engine, lubricant,* or *motive.* Studies of *arrestees* may not be particularly relevant in this sphere. The acquisition of controlled dangerous substances through the proceeds of robbery or of property crime more convincingly portrays drugs as "motive" than as "engine." Since there is no particularly strong reason to believe that drug-positive arrestees were actively "under the influence" when a crime was committed, it may be the case that they behaved criminally quite independently of what McGlothlin has called direct pharmacological influence; but there is no particular reason to believe that, either. Only the Census study, replete with all the faults of self-report methodology and retrospective self-portrayal, but which nonetheless asked directly for a self-assessment of whether the respondent was actively "under the influence" at the time of the instant offense, responds to the question of whether controlled dangerous substances "trigger" felony crime *either* as engine or lubricant. In view of the virtual impossibility of obtaining laboratory-analyzable data at or near the point of commission of a crime, one might well be forced to "settle" for the self-report data of convicted felons (who, after all, no longer have a strong stake in dissembling) as the most defensible approximation to a "base rate" representing whether *biochemistry in fact dictated criminal behavior in an instant offense*. Alternately, however, convicted felons may have a relatively strong motive for retrospective exculpation by off-loading personal guilt onto drug use. However that may be, the relevant data suggest that something on the order of one in three felony crimes, whether of violence or against property, were at the least "lubricated" if not indeed engendered by drug use or abuse.

Future inquiry will rely heavily on the "hard sciences." Quite clearly, however, the current state of research does not yet permit anything resembling *differential* conclusions about *which* substances accelerate *what* crimes. That remains for future inquiry; and one might confidently expect that the "hard sciences" of biochemistry and neuropsychopharmacology will take the lead in the next round of investigations.

"Pathological intoxication" legislation, bandwidth infidelity in drug testing, and the growth of the "designer drug" industry collide to produce a forensic Wonderland. Finally, it has been observed that adoption by state legislatures of an American Psychiatric Association-endorsed "amendment" to legislation on diminished responsibility which excludes "voluntary ingestion" of alcohol and/or psychoactive substances as a basis for pleading diminished responsibility, increased concern in the community of biomedical scientists about "bandwidth fidelity" in drug testing, and the rapid upsurge in the manufacture of mood-altering drugs which sets out to avoid "controlled, dangerous" ingredients by "drug designers," producing in the process substances that evade laboratory detection, create a forensic Wonderland for clinician and attorney.

REFERENCES

American Psychiatric Association, Statement on the Insanity Defense. *Issues in Forensic Psychiatry* (Washington: American Psychiatric Press, 1984).
Bureau of Justice Statistics, *Profile of Jail Inmates: National Prisoner Statistics Report SD NPS J-6, NCJ-65412.* (Washington: U.S. Department of Justice, 1980). Pp. 9, 17-21.

Collins, James J., Jr. Alcohol Careers and Criminal Careers. In James J. Collins, Jr. (ed.), *Drinking and Crime* (New York: Guilford, 1981). Pp. 152-206.

Dwyer, Richard E. The Employer's Need to Provide a Safe Working Environment: Use and Abuse of Drug Screening. *Labor Studies Journal*, 1988, 12, 3-19.

Finkle, Bryan S. and Kevin L. McCloskey, The Forensic Toxicology of Cocaine, *National Institute on Drug Abuse Research Monograph Series 13: Cocaine*. (Washington: NIDA, 1977).

Graham, Mary D. Controlling Drug Abuse and Crime: A Research Update. *NIJ Reports/SNI 202*, March-April 1987, pp. 2-7.

Hofmann, Frederick G. and Adele D. Hofmann, *A Handbook on Drug and Alcohol Abuse: The Biomedical Aspects*. (New York: Oxford University Press, 1975).

Jackson, George W. Substance Abuse: Special Issue, *Seminars in Occupational Medicine*, 1986, 1, 4 (Entire issue).

McGarrell, Edmund F. and Timothy J. Flanagan, *Sourcebook of Criminal Justice Statistics* (Washington: Bureau of Justice Statistics, U.S. Department of Justice, 1985).

McGlothin, William H. Distinguishing Effects from Concomitants of Drug Use: The Case of Crime. In Lee N. Robins (ed.), *Studying Drug Abuse: Series in Psychosocial Epidemiology, VI* (New Brunswick: Rutgers University Press, 1985). Pp. 153-172.

Perry, Samuel. Substance-induced Organic Mental Disorders. In Robert E. Hales & Stuart C. Yudofsky (eds.), *Textbook of Neuropsychiatry* (Washington: American Psychiatric Association, 1987). Pp. 157-176.

Peterson, Donald R. The Role of Assessment in Professional Psychology. In Donald R. Peterson and Daniel B. Fishman (eds.), *Assessment for Decision*. (New Brunswick: Rutgers University Press, 1987). Pp. 5-43.

Prisoners and Drugs, Bulletin NCJ-875752. (Washington: Bureau of Justice Statistics, U. S. Department of Justice, 1983).

Profile of Jail Inmates: National Prisoner Statistics Report SD NPS J-6, NCJ-65412. (Washington: Bureau of Justice Statistics, U.S. Department of Justice, 1980).

Richardson, Philip, Mark J. Morein, and John G. Phin. *Criminal Justice Drug Abuse Surveillance System* (Arlington: Special Studies Division, Creative SocioMedics, 1978).

Roizen, Judy. Alcohol and Criminal Behavior among Blacks: The Case for Research on Special Populations. In James J. Collins, Jr. (ed.), *Drinking and Crime* (New York: Guilford, 1981). Pp. 207-252.

Schatzberg, Alan F. and Jonathan O. Cole. *Manual of Clinical Psychopharmacology* (Washington: American Psychiatric Association, 1986).

Toborg, Mary A. and John P. Bellassai. *Assessment of Pretrial Urine Testing in the District of Columbia, I: Background and Description of the Urine Testing Program; IV: Analysis of Drug Use Among Arrestees* (Washington: Toborg Associates, 1987).

Wish, Eric D., Elizabeth Brady, and Mary Cuadrado. *Urine Testing of Arrestees: Findings from Manhattan* (New York: Narcotic and Drug Research, Inc., 1986).

Wish, Eric D. *Drug Use in Arrestees in Manhattan: The Dramatic Increase in Cocaine from 1984 to 1986* (New York: Narcotic and Drug Research Inc., 1987).

Outpatient Treatment
for Substance-Abusing Offenders

J. David Hirschel
Janet R. Keny

The "war on drugs" has been waged for some decades now, but we appear no closer to winning this war today than we have ever been. Indeed, to some we seem to be continually losing ground in the battle. Frustration with present efforts has led to some radical proposals. Recently the Mayors of Baltimore, Maryland, and Charles Town, West Virginia, have led a call for a national debate on decriminalizing illegal narcotics (Saundra, 1988).

The statistics on illegal drug use are not encouraging. Research on young adults in the United States indicates that: "By their mid-twenties, nearly 80% of today's young adults have tried an *illicit drug*, including some 60% who have tried some *illicit drug other than* (usually in addition to) *marijuana*" (National Institute on Drug Abuse, 1987, p. 23). Furthermore, over 90% of high school seniors report having used alcohol, with some two-thirds having imbibed within the month prior to the survey (National Institute on Drug Abuse, 1987, pp. 29, 110).

The problems engendered by substance abuse are manifold. The individual abuser may face physical, psychological, social, and financial problems as a result of substance abuse. Psychological and physical addiction are real threats, as are a host of other types of physical ills from lesions of the skin, damage to the membranes of the nose, and cirrhosis of the liver to death from AIDS or from a contaminated or unexpectedly pure batch of drugs. Involvement in

---

J. David Hirschel, PhD, is Professor of Criminal Justice at the University of North Carolina, Charlotte.

Janet R. Keny, MS, is consultant to the Drug Education Center, Charlotte.

drug abuse may result in the disruption of social bonds and the loss of a job or the shattering of employment opportunities. Either through use of the drugs themselves, by committing crimes while under the influence of the drugs, or by committing crimes to acquire money to obtain drugs, the abuser may run foul of the law.

Nor will the ills attendant upon substance abuse rest with the abuser alone. Family members will rarely be able to remain immune from the problems presented by this abuse. Denial of a problem, a hallmark of addiction, is seen in family members as well as in the chemically dependent person. Indeed, families often adapt to the negative changes in behavior of a substance abuser, unwittingly enabling the abuse to continue. At best the family will have to cope with the strain presented by an uncooperative and unproductive family member. At worst the family may have to face physical danger and incur financial and legal liabilities as a result of the abuser's actions.

At a more general level, substance abuse constitutes an enormous drain on the nation's economy, and on the resources of social, welfare, treatment, and criminal justice agencies. It has been estimated that the nation faces a "$59 billion annual toll exacted by illegal drug use and related crime" (Graham, 1987, p. 2). And this does not include the costs incurred as a result of alcohol abuse. While the burdens of substance abuse are felt by a host of government agencies, in the "war on drugs" the power of the criminal justice system has, in particular, been summoned to combat the enemy.

The United States has in general taken what has been termed a "law enforcement" approach toward overcoming the problems of substance abuse (Barbara & Morrison, 1975). The failure of Prohibition resulted in the legalization of alcohol. A similar lack of success by the criminal justice system in curbing drug abuse has, as has already been noted, resulted in a call from some quarters for a similar resolution. Others, however, believe that efforts at preventing the importation of illegal drugs, and the domestic cultivation, manufacture, and sale of such substances, should simply be strengthened.

Action is also being taken to inhibit drug-taking behavior before it begins, through the establishment of drug and alcohol abuse prevention programs. As the greatest surge in initial drug use occurs between the seventh and eighth grades (S. Kim, 1987), primary prevention programs are now being aimed at elementary school students, particularly those in the fifth and sixth grades. However, since it has been observed that incarcerated substance abusers perceive drug taking as less harmful than does the average high school senior (Mabli et al., 1985), it is uncertain what effect such prevention and early intervention exert on the high risk populations that inhabit our prisons and are to be found more generally in the criminal justice system.

Although a great many substance abusers escape the clutches of the criminal law, the numbers processed by the criminal justice system are still extremely high. For example, in 1986 alone some four million persons were arrested for drug and alcohol offenses (824,100 for drug abuse violations, 933,900 for drunkenness, 1,793,300 for driving under the influence, and 600,200 for liquor law violations) (Federal Bureau of Investigation, 1987, p. 164). Moreover these numbers tell only part of the story; for, they deal only with offenders who have been arrested for direct violations of drug and alcohol laws. They say nothing about offenders who have committed other offenses either under the influence of, or because of, a mood altering substance. Current research indicates that these cases are also extremely numerous. Thus, drug testing of male arrestees in Manhattan revealed that 56% of those arrested in 1984, and over 75% of those arrested in 1986, tested positive for opiate, cocaine, PCP, or methadone use. About 25% tested positive for multiple drug use (Wish, 1987). These findings confirm the results of earlier studies (see e.g., Bureau of Narcotics and Dangerous Drugs, 1971; U.S. Department of Justice, 1983-b), and are supported by the results of other recent studies conducted in other locales (see e.g., Graham, 1987).

The orientation of the criminal law is to hold offenders directly responsible for their violations of the law and to punish them for those violations. Although rehabilitation of the offender is one of the rationales taken into consideration when sentencing a convicted offender, it is not the sole, or perhaps even the primary, rationale. Thus, when a convicted substance abuser has been sentenced for a criminal offense, he/she may not receive treatment for the substance abuse problem. Surveys conducted on incarcerated offenders indicate widespread substance abuse, but little treatment for it. Thus, one survey disclosed that almost a third of all state prisoners had committed their crimes while under the influence of drugs, that more than half had taken drugs during the month just prior to the crime, and that more than three-quarters had used drugs at some time during their lives, but that "only one-fourth of the drug users had ever been in a drug treatment program" (U.S. Department of Justice, 1983-b, p. 1). A second survey yielded similar result with regard to alcohol abusers (U.S. Department of Justice, 1983-a). Yet one study of alcoholic bank robbers concluded that immediate attention to treatment of the alcoholism is so crucial to reducing recidivism that such treatment should be mandated for offenders on prison pre-release or probation or parole (Lieberman and Haran, 1985).

Although there is a wide variety of drug treatment programs in correctional institutions, the setting and atmosphere under which they are conducted may not be very treatment oriented. As a reviewer of correctional drug treatment programs has concluded: "the limited data that are available is not supportive of treatment of addiction in a prison setting" (Petersen, 1974, p. 151). With concern voiced about lack of suitable treatment in penal settings, it has been suggested that the criminal law approach tends to foster a cycle of "addiction — arrest — release — readiction — rearrest" (U.S. Department of Justice, 1979, p. 4).

The criminal law is not, however, the only mechanism for providing citizens with treatment for substance abuse problems. Such individuals may seek out treatment on their own. In addition, the civil law provides for treatment at public expense on either a voluntary or involuntary basis. These civil commitment procedures, which are often tied in with the process for civil commitment of the mentally ill, do not, however, generally apply to the casual user. Their provisions usually extend only to addicts, or to addicts and those in imminent danger of becoming addicts.

Given the concern about the inability of the criminal justice system to provide adequate treatment for substance abusers, such offenders have often been diverted from the criminal justice system (see e.g., Weissman, 1979). Increasingly nowadays, however, treatment is being sought as part of the criminal justice system processing. One program that attempts to achieve this is the Treatment Alternatives to Street Crime (TASC) program, which identifies criminal offenders with drug problems and refers them for treatment while still retaining jurisdiction over them. The focus is primarily on nonviolent property criminals who commit these crimes in order to support their habits. The philosophy behind the program is that if one deals directly with the underlying problem of drug abuse, future involvement in criminal activity will be lessened. Other more traditional ways of providing offenders with treatment include, as discussed above, providing such treatment in correctional institutions, and mandating treatment as a condition of probation, parole, or deferred prosecution. It has been suggested that with the advent of TASC "probations became more attractive as sentencing options for the judiciary" (System Sciences, 1978, p. 4).

The criminal justice system has increasingly been turning to treatment agencies for assistance in dealing with substance abusing offenders. With the move toward alternatives to incarceration, this has tended to mean providing these offenders with treatment in the community. Other developments, such as the campaign against drunk driving, have also impacted upon the demand for these treatment resources.

At the same time as this has been occurring in the criminal justice system, there has been a general move in the field of substance abuse treatment toward dealing with clients in an outpatient as opposed to an inpatient setting (Knowles, 1983; Singh et al., 1982). A variety of factors, such as cost and the ability of the patient to maintain a job and other relationships in the community (Knowles, 1983, p. 385), account for this trend. Of assistance to the outpatient protagonists is the allegation that there is no "overall agreement that either setting is superior to the other" (Chernus, 1985, p. 69). What may be lost, however, in an outpatient setting is the ability of the treatment staff to provide intense therapy and continuous support services, and to monitor the progress of the client closely. The outpatient client, in addition, does not enjoy the immediate presence of a support group or the safety of a secure setting where feelings of anxiety and vulnerability, emotions common to the recovery process, can be experienced without the danger of relapse.

The trend, then, is toward increased involvement of criminal offenders in substance abuse treatment programs, and more outpatient treatment for substance abusers in general. As the numbers of criminal justice referred clients increase among the caseloads of these treatment agencies, a number of crucial issues emerge for consideration. First, how do these criminal justice referred clients perform in treatment? Second, what is the impact of these clients upon the operation of the treatment agencies? And, third, what does the experience gained from dealing with criminal justice referred clients teach us for the future?

APPRAISAL OF TREATMENT PERFORMANCE

There is a wide variety of outpatient substance abuse treatment programs throughout the nation. These range from methadone maintenance clinics to detoxification and drug free outpatient units. The latter may range from highly structured therapies for abusers and their families to somewhat unstructured programs, such as drop-in centers, aimed at high risk youth. Residential programs vary in length of stay from the short time required to safely detoxify the user to months or even years of intense involvement in a closed-unit structured therapeutic community followed by gradual re-entry into society via a half-way house residential program. Increasingly, both outpatient drug-free and residential programs utilize group therapy as the core of treatment. The 12-step program developed by Alcoholics Anonymous and Alateen (teens in alcoholic families) is both a concurrent and follow-up resource for users in treatment. This model utilizes group confrontation and can, through special needs groups, such as Narcotics Anonymous, Cocaine Anonymous and Alateen, address specific issues raised by the wide variety of chemically dependent persons that exist in our society.

Substance abuse programs receive their clients from a large number of referral sources. Some clients may be self-referrals, motivated by their own desire to change, buttressed on occasion by pressure from family members. Others may be referred by employers or school officials. Others may be ordered into treatment as a result of invocation of the civil commitment process. Still others may be sent for treatment as part of their processing through the criminal justice system.

Leverage to remain in, and successfully complete, treatment can be observed whenever there is a third-party involved in the referral process. Speaking from his own experience working with clients in narcotic addiction and alcohol treatment programs, Berlinger (1987) notes "the rarity with which substance abusers spontaneously move toward reorganizing their lives" and the need for "some form of compulsion to get their attention" (p. 4).

While there may be no legal consequences to failure in treatment for a non-court involved user, a husband, wife or employer can exert great influence and leverage over a client through the social, family and financial consequences that attend abandonment of the treatment program. Strug and Hyman (1981) call attention to the significant role played by members of an alcoholic's social network in bringing the client to treatment, and underscore the importance of identifying significant others who can cooperate with treatment staff in the treatment program. The concept of "constructive coercion," whereby "a patient's future employment (is made) contingent on active participation in alcoholism or drug rehabilitation programs" (Ward, 1982, p. 2) has been used in the workplace with a great measure of success (Trice & Beyer, 1982).

Family involvement in treatment of a criminal justice referred client may result in an added element of leverage. Relatives who learn how to avoid "enabling" behaviors may threaten to take out a warrant if the user steals from a family member rather than "keeping the problem in the family" as is so often the reaction of families with drug abusing members. A user who knows his family will not tolerate illegal behavior, but rather will have him re-arrested and face incarceration, is logically more highly motivated to try to "work his program" and succeed in treatment. There is, indeed, a growing consensus among treatment professionals that leverage is a valuable aid not only in bringing a denying user into treatment, but also in keeping that user involved until the ever-present denial is diminished and the problems of addiction are addressed.

While family, employer, or court involvement may provide the stimulus to bring a user into treatment, the most therapeutically comprehensive programs do not let go of the referral source after the client has been admitted into a treatment program. Family therapy is a growing addition to other group therapy modalities in both outpatient and residential programs (National Institute on Drug Abuse, 1985). Clients in DWI schools have even been offered rebates for bringing family members or significant others to family education programs (McGrath, 1986). Employers and school personnel may also be brought in to help set goals in treatment and establish consequences for failing to meet such goals. TASC clients in treatment are closely monitored by a variety of staff. Though treated primarily in group therapy, each drug abuse client will receive an individualized treatment program which will vary according to the client's needs and resources. Even after the completion of a formal treatment program, the continued involvement of these third parties can have a significant impact on the client's success in maintaining recovery.

While clients in substance abuse treatment programs differ with regard to the source of their referral for treatment, they vary in other significant ways too. There will be variation in the type of drug abused, whether there is polydrug use, whether there are concomitant physical or psychological problems, the existence of marital or other family difficulties, and the presence of employment problems.

To some the focus on the prior criminality of a segment of the treatment population may appear unwarranted. After all, the function of the treatment program is to take care of the substance abuse problem. Involvement in crime is just one factor to be taken into account in devising an appropriate treatment plan for the client. Moreover it may not be as important a factor as, for example, psychopathology, which, it has been suggested, has been much neglected in substance abuse treatment research (Jaffe, 1984). In addition, it may be argued that a great number of substance abusers by the very act of taking drugs are committing criminal offenses and that, with so many offenders escaping apprehension and conviction, it may be just a matter of chance as to which client ends up as a criminal justice system referral.

To drug treatment personnel unaccustomed to dealing with criminal justice referred clients who are on probation or parole, the specter of an influx of such clients may be alarming. They may be projected as more difficult, perhaps potentially violent clients, who will not only fare badly in treatment themselves, but also adversely affect the successful treatment potential of other clients.

The results of research studies conducted on the treatment performance of criminal justice referred clients, though somewhat equivocal, do not in general provide support for these fears. However, it must be borne in mind that there are difficulties comparing the results of studies that focus upon different types of subjects and employ different outcome measures. In addition, many of the studies that have been conducted are methodologically flawed for such reasons as failure to account for selection bias and sample attrition (Dunham & Mauss, 1982, pp. 8-9). In his review of the early studies on the effect of legal coercion on the treatment of alcoholism, Ward (1979) concluded that although most of the studies found that coercion worked, their "conclusions were unwarranted based on the research designs" (p. 396). Typical methodological problems cited included "the absence of control groups, . . . and ambiguous criteria for validly measuring treatment success" (p. 396).

In their own study, in which they controlled for ten socio-demographic variables, Dunham and Mauss (1982) discovered that problem drinkers coerced into outpatient treatment by the courts were considerably more likely than strictly voluntary referrals to have successful treatment outcomes. Likewise, Salmon (1982) found that the legal coercion provided by criminal justice system involvement "facilitate(d) success for older longer term addicts, by the criteria of arrest and abstinence, in drug free settings" (p. 65). Finally, Collins and Allison (1983) report from their examination of data collected in the national Treatment Outcome Prospective Study (TOPS) that drug abusers who were legally coerced into treatment performed as well as voluntary clients on a number of outcome measures.

On the other side of the issue, however, Harford et al. (1976) found that although legal pressure had motivated many of the criminal justice system clients to apply for treatment, there was no evidence that this pressure improved either the rate of retention or the probability of successful program completion. Examining the longer term effects of treatment participation, Simpson (1984) observes from his review of data obtained on clients in the national Drug Abuse Reporting Program (DARP) that "higher rates of preadmission arrests and incarcerations were related to poorer post-treatment outcomes" (p. 33). As Jaffe sums it up: "Those with the highest levels of criminality prior to seeking treatment continue to represent a challenge to our capacity to alter behavior" (1984, p. 14).

Retention of clients in treatment is perhaps the greatest difficulty facing outpatient substance abuse treatment programs. Here there is evidence to suggest that the added element of legal coercion may provide a client the added impetus required to promote his/her staying in the program. Thus, Collins and Allison (1983) found that drug abusers who had been legally coerced into treatment remained longer in treatment than voluntary clients. Most successful were those (namely the TASC clients) whose participation was closely monitored. Steer (1983) noted a positive correlation between retention in drug free counseling and referral for treatment by the judicial system. Kofoed et al. (1986) likewise discovered that for clients with substance abuse and coexisting psychiatric disorders there was a positive relationship between legal coercion and retention in treatment. As they point out: "Legal contingencies may be particularly important bargaining chips in obtaining treatment compliance and sobriety in patients who are isolated from the usual social forces that influence patients to accept treatment" (p. 870). In addiction, it should be noted that involvement in the criminal justice system may help indicate to the client the gravity of the substance abuse problem, making up for an element which it has been suggested accompanies inpatient, but not outpatient, treatment (Bonstedt et al., 1984, p. 1039). The importance of retaining clients in treatment is underscored by the finding that "time in treatment — regardless of modality/environment — has been shown to be positively related to outcome" (Allison and Hubbard, 1985, p. 1334).

Contrary to initial projections, court referred clients may, then, not be entering treatment accompanied by a host of additional problems that impact negatively upon their treatment performance. Anecdotal reports from both alcohol and polydrug treatment programs buttress the overall findings of these research studies, and by describing the treatment process provide an analytical explanation for this outcome. Central to this explanation are the initial attitudinal differences that exist between voluntary and court-refered (both

TASC and probation and parole-involved) clients. The voluntary, self-referred, clients often see themselves as somehow different or special, having had the "insight" to come voluntarily to a treatment program. They frequently hide behind a huge wall of denial, imagining their life situations and chemical use to be "better" than, or "different" from, those of the court involved clients. As a result, these clients may withdraw from treatment when their denial is confronted in group therapy and they realize their real situation may well be identical to that of the leveraged client. Court involved users, on the other hand, are reported as frequently negative and resentful at intake and the early stages of therapy. This energy, when exhibited in a negative fashion, is also a form of denial, but can be transformed into positive energy for recovery and honest assessment when the client faces the alternative of incarceration. Leverage can, then, be used to keep a client in treatment long enough to progress past denial and face the tasks that must be confronted in treatment.

IMPACT UPON TREATMENT AGENCIES

Criminal justice referred clients have, then, fared considerably better in treatment than projected. However, it is not only their performance in treatment that must be considered. Of concern too is the impact they may have upon other clients in the programs to which they are admitted.

Overall, research studies and anecdotal feedback indicate that the addition of criminal justice referred clients has not had a negative impact on the treatment programs. In their examination of the impact of the implementation of a TASC project on drug treatment program objectives and operations, Hirschel and McCarthy (1984) found that, despite a change in the size and composition of the treatment population, the influx of TASC clients did not in any way inhibit the effective treatment of the other clients. Indeed, there were indications that, perhaps as a result of tighter surveillance and control, the non-criminal justice referred clients were actually performing better in treatment after the introduction of the TASC clients.

Despite the fact that the presence of criminal justice referred clients does not appear to have an overall negative effect on the performance of other clients, the admission of these clients does give rise to some program management issues.

One issue that has been raised relates to the influence such clients can exert on group therapy when the group is composed primarily of criminal justice referred clients. With the treatment focus on group therapy and the unique commonalities of experience among former inmates, there exists the danger of treatment time being diverted to legal issues if there is a majority of criminal justice referred clients in the group. When they form a minority in a group, their colleagues in treatment can moderate this variation of denial and keep them focused on the tasks of recovery and success, essentially saying: "We don't care what got you here. We care how you're doing now and where you'll be in the future."

This potential negative influence on group therapy has, however, been considered more of a problem with residential as opposed to outpatient programs. As a result, residential treatment facilities often limit the percentage of criminal justice referred clients in their programs at any given time. Furthermore, some residential programs require that parolees participate in an outpatient program before being accepted into an inpatient facility. However, outpatient programs have not felt the need to limit the percentage of court referred clients in any given group.

Clients who are on methadone pose a similar problem for group therapy since, unlike other clients who are urged to be drug free and adopt lifestyles that do not involve chemical escape or recreation, they are legally provided with drugs. Not surprisingly they are steadfast in their refusal to stop taking methadone, and will indeed fight to remain on it. The consequence is that their own personal goals may be in conflict with those of the treatment agency and its other clients. To dilute the negative impact of these clients, they are generally placed, regardless of the referral source, in groups with other drug abusing clients rather than in a methadone only group in the hope that they too will adopt the therapeutic goal of living drug free.

A second management issue that evolves from admitting criminal justice referred clients into treatment programs concerns the punishment/treatment dichotomy. Criminal justice referrals, especially if they are accompanied by probation or parole supervision, carry at the very least an implication of a punishment orientation. This manifests itself in at least two ways. The first relates to monitoring and surveillance techniques that may be routinely used in the criminal justice system, but may be considered deleterious in a treatment setting. Probation and Parole officials have always had to strike a balance between acting as a friend of the client and serving as a monitoring and surveillance agent for the court. Treatment officials, on the other hand, are unaccustomed to adopting such conflicting roles.

To aid in the monitoring function, a number of testing techniques are currently being used to detect substance abuse. These include the breathalyzer and urinalysis. Of prime concern here, because of its common usage and obtrusive nature, is urinalysis.

Because of the interrelationship between drugs and crime, the routine drug testing of arrestees has been advocated and in fact implemented in some jurisdictions (Graham, 1987). For those offenders with substance abuse problems, continued testing is seen as a desirable feature of a treatment-rehabilitation program. Since the offender is at least in part being punished for his offense, no further justification is required for the intrusion that drug testing may involve in his/her life.

For drug treatment programs, on the other hand, the rationale of punishment cannot be used to justify such intrusion. However, drug testing, and in particular urinalysis, have in recent years become more routine features of these programs. In a growing number of inpatient and outpatient programs, clients must agree to submit to urinalysis as part of the treatment contract as well as the intake process. Urinalysis is standardly undertaken for detection of narcotics, marijuana, cocaine, amphetamines, and barbiturates. It is most common for a client to be given twenty-four hour notice for submitting to urinalysis. Failure to submit to testing is considered tantamount to providing a "dirty" urine (urine showing the presence of an illicit drug in the user's system).

While most programs that utilize urinalysis first perform the procedure upon intake into treatment as a routine matter to establish a baseline of current drug use, the decision of whether to require a subsequent test is usually left to the discretion of the counselor

working with the client. The criterion utilized in making this decision is the client's overall performance in treatment, not the need to
provide continual monitoring of the client's activities. The counselor considers the client's drug and alcohol history, reports of re-
lapses from outside sources such as group or family members and
overall treatment response when determining whether to order urinalysis. Testing can be particularly effective when a "dirty" urine
is returned on a client who is continuing to deny not only current
drug use, but even the existence of any problem with chemical dependency. The seemingly irrefutable evidence provided by a
"dirty" urine can be used to break through continued denial and
enhance progress in treatment.

From a therapeutic standpoint, urinalysis is most effectively performed when the client can experience the consequences of a
"dirty" urine as quickly as possible. The ideal maximum turn-
around time for urinalysis results is forty-eight hours (Bureau of
Justice Assistance, 1988). Unfortunately, many treatment programs
have urinalysis test results taking four or five days to be returned
and then shared with clients. For this procedure to be most effective
in helping modify behaviors, it must be done in an expedient fashion.

The one exception to counselor discretion on the use of urinalysis
occurs when the client is on methadone. In this case drug testing is
mandated by federal regulations. A methadone client must undergo
a minimum of eight random tests during the first year of maintenance, and at least one every three months thereafter (Federal Register for Federal Treatment Standards for Methadone Programs,
Section 291.505,d-4). There is a twofold purpose for this testing: to
ensure that the client is not using other drugs which in combination
with methadone might be life-threatening; and to ascertain that the
client does indeed have methadone in his/her system.

Not only do chemical dependency programs require that their
clients abstain from drug use, they also now most commonly require alcohol abstinence as well. Alcohol treatment programs have
long required a total abstinence agreement by clients, but some drug
treatment centers were not as quick to outlaw the use of alcohol. A
very real problem in dealing with court involved clients arises from

the fact that alcohol is not an illegal drug, and that unless so specified as a condition of probation or parole, clients who use alcohol
do not face the same consequences as when they take other drugs.
In addition, the urine test for alcohol is far more expensive than for
other drugs and is not standardly used in the drug screen in urinalysis. Therefore clients may well be using significant quantities of
alcohol which go undetected by the most common urinalyses employed. It has even been suggested that a client may come in with a
cocaine problem and leave with an alcohol problem instead.

The second aspect of the conflict between punishment and treatment involves perhaps the most crucial issue of all: the measure-
ment of both failure and success in treatment. What may constitute
failure from a criminal justice perspective may not be so regarded
from a treatment perspective. Thus, for example, any use of illicit
drugs is a violation of the conditions of probation or parole, and
subjects the violator to revocation and incarceration, certain signs
of failure. From a treatment perspective, however, this may not be
regarded as a failure, especially if the client has maintained a long
period of abstinence and is showing insight into his/her problems.
Since relapse may be anticipated on the road to recovery, it may be
argued that as long as the periods between use of illicit drugs are
growing longer a client can be regarded as making progress in treatment, and should not be labelled as a failure. The practical problem
that arises here involves the conflict that can occur between treatment staff and criminal justice officials, both of whom have responsibility for overseeing the client.

Court referred clients must frequently have the results of urinalyses sent to their probation/parole officers, particularly if a condition of probation/parole is that the offender remain drug free. TASC
clients, who are the most rigorously monitored of all clients in treatment, will always have the results of their urinalyses shared with
their TASC counselors and probation officers. If a "dirty" urine is
an indication of a probation violation, then the offender in treatment
may indeed face the consequence of being incarcerated as a result of
providing a "dirty" urine. However, treatment professionals report
that it is rare to terminate any client from treatment as a result of a

first, or even a second, "dirty" urine. Relapse is expected as part of the recovery process, and urinalysis indicating relapse is used as therapeutically as possible, and not punitively. Most treatment issues are not as black and white as the result of a urine test.

As a consequence, treatment professionals report some frustration with the very tangible nature of urinalysis and its impact on court involved clients if a "dirty" urine is given. The problem appears to be that corrections and other criminal justice officials have not been fully educated with regard to the implications of its use both in treatment and as a probation/parole monitoring tool. Treatment is a qualitative process. The quantitative test of urinalysis is frequently welcomed by court officials in determining the success of the qualitative and somewhat elusive process of chemical dependency treatment. Ironically, as noted above, a failed urine test, which could help send an offender to prison, can also be a positive occurrence in a client's treatment, aiding him/her to break through denial. Not surprisingly, chemical dependency counselors tend to believe that educating judges and corrections officials about this situation constitutes a crucial task that must be accomplished.

The criminal justice referred clients have another major impact on the treatment programs that cannot be ignored. Not only do they help the programs maintain adequate numbers of fee-paying clients in treatment, but they also bring in government money to support the programs. As Hunsaker (1986) points out: "Many substance abuse programs can benefit financially by increasing their referrals from the criminal justice system" (p. 1832). He regards criminal justice referred clients as having "a high probability of remitting fees, since they can avoid further litigation by complying with program requirements" (1986, p. 1831), and proposes a technique for increasing the referral rate of criminal justice clients by offering counselors "commissions" based on patient fees. Open House, Inc., of Charlotte, North Carolina, a multi-faceted drug treatment program, reports that TASC and criminal justice involved clients, both residential and drug-free outpatient, in addition to staying in treatment longer, pay client fees more regularly than do voluntary clients.

The focus on providing treatment for drunk drivers has provided a possible financial boon for treatment agencies with a "potentially large amount of money to be made by charging assessment and program fees" (Rosenberg & Spiller, 1986, p. 166). Program administrators do, however, need to be wary of the conflict of interests that can arise between a client's treatment needs and the financial concerns of the program and its counselors.

IMPLICATIONS FOR THE FUTURE

For substance abuse treatment centers faced with the prospects of criminal justice referred clients entering their programs, the prognosis is in general a good one. Contrary to expectations, these clients do not tend to perform less well in treatment than other clients. Both the leverage that is exerted over them as a result of their involvement in the criminal justice system, and the added surveillance and monitoring that they receive as a consequence, are significant factors contributing to their ability to remain, and perform well, in treatment. The benefits of leverage as a therapeutic tool have long been recognized. Just as leverage exerted by family and employers can have a positive influence on clients, so can the leverage generated by their involvement with the criminal justice system. The additional surveillance and monitoring they receive can likewise be used for therapeutic ends, especially in helping treatment staff confront and break down the denial that is such a common obstacle in chemical dependency.

Not only do the criminal justice clients perform well in treatment themselves; they also have little negative impact on other clients in the treatment programs. Indeed, there are indications that these other clients are benefitting from the admission of criminal justice clients, primarily as a result of the added attention they too may receive.

Financial advantages also accrue for the treatment programs. In addition to bringing government dollars into the programs, criminal justice system referred clients who pay for treatment services have in general shown themselves to have a better fee payment history than other clients. This may again be attributable to the leverage that is exerted over them as a result of their involvement in the criminal justice system.

The single major problem encountered involves the definition of the concepts of success and failure. The conflict between criminal justice officials and treatment professionals over whether a relapse constitutes failure needs to be addressed. From a treatment perspective, it would be desirable for criminal justice officials to allow a client some relapse during treatment, without automatically resorting to probation or parole revocation and consequent incarceration. One solution might be to have conditions of probation and parole written to require compliance with treatment program conditions, rather than total abstinence from drug use. Of course every effort would have to be taken to ensure that clients were not led to believe that continued drug use was being condoned. Since drug use could still lead to program termination and probation or parole revocation, this would not seem to be a difficult task to accomplish.

REFERENCES

Allison, M., & Hubbard, R.L. (1985). Drug Abuse treatment process: A review of the literature. *The International Journal of the Addictions, 20*(9), 1321-1345.

Barbara, J., & Morrison, J. (1975). If addiction is incurable, why do we try to cure it? A comparison of control methods in the U.K. and the U.S. *Crime and Delinquency, 21*, 28-33.

Berlinger, A.K. (1987). Group counseling with alcohol offenders: An analysis and typology of DWI probationers. *Journal of Offender Counseling, Services & Rehabilitation, 11*(2), 33-51.

Bronstedt, T., Ulrich, D.A., Dolinar, L.J., & Johnson, J.J. (1984). When and where should we hospitalize alcoholics? *Hospital and Community Psychiatry, 35*(10), 1038-1040.

Bureau of Justice Assistance, U.S. Department of Justice. (1988). *Urinalysis as a part of a Treatment Alternatives to Street Crime Program*. Washington, DC: Author.

Bureau of Narcotics and Dangerous Drugs, U.S. Department of Justice. (1971). *Drug usage and arrest charges: A study of drug usage and arrest charges among arrestees in six metropolitan areas of the United States*. Washington, DC: Author.

Chernus, L.A. (1985). Clinical issues in alcoholism treatment. *The Journal of Contemporary Social Work*, 67-75.

Collins, J. J., & Allison, M. (1983). Legal coercion and treatment for drug abuse. *Hospital and Community Psychiatry, 34*(12), 1145-1149.

Dunham, R.G. & Mauss, A.L. (1982). Reluctant referrals: The effectiveness of legal coercion in outpatient treatment for problem drinkers. *Journal of Drug Issues, 12*, 5-20.

Federal Bureau of Investigation, U.S. Department of Justice. (1987). *Uniform crime reports: Crime in the United States-1986.* Washington, DC: U.S. Government Printing Office.

Graham, M. G. (March/April 1987). Controlling drug abuse and crime: A research update. *NIJ Reports*, 2-7.

Harford, R.J., Ungerer, M.A. & Kinsella, J.K. (1976). Effects of legal pressure on prognosis for treatment of drug dependence. *American Journal of Psychiatry, 133*, 1399-1404.

Hirschel, J.D. & McCarthy, B.R. (1984). The TASC-drug treatment program connection: Cooperation, cooption, or corruption of treatment objectives? *Journal of Offender Counseling, Services & Rehabilitation, 8*(1/2), 117-130.

Hunsaker, A.C. (1986). The effect of a contingent monetary reward on probation referrals to a drug abuse program. *The International Journal of the Addictions, 20*, 1831-35.

Jaffe, J.H. (1984). Evaluating drug abuse treatment: A comment on the state of the art. In National Institute on Drug Abuse. *Research Monograph 51: Drug abuse treatment evaluation: Strategies, progress, and prospects* (pp. 13-28). Rockville, MD. Author.

Kim, S., Crutchfield, C., & Newman, S.H. (1987). *Drug Abuse by Students in Mecklenburg County, N.C.: Main Findings, 1986.* Charlotte, NC: Drug Education Center.

Kofoed, L., Kania, J., Walsh, T., & Atkinson, R.M. (1986). Outpatient treatment of patients with substance abuse and coexisting psychiatric disorders. *American Journal of Psychiatry, 143*(7), 867-872.

Knowles, P.L. (1983). Inpatient versus outpatient treatment of substance misuse in hospitals, 1975-1979. *Journal of Studies on Alcohol, 44*(2), 384-387.

Liebermhn, L., & Haran, J.F. (1985). Alcoholic bank robber. *Federal Probation, 49*(2), 45-49.

Mabli, J., Nesbitt, K.L., Glick, S., Tilbrook, J., & Coldwell, B. (1985). FCI Fort Worth substance abuse evaluation: A pilot study. *Federal Probation, 49*(3), 40-45.

McGrath, R.J. (1986). An education program for collateral of DWI offenders. In S.K. Valle (Ed.). *Drunk driving in America: Strategies and approaches to treatment.* NY: The Haworth Press.

National Institute on Drug Abuse. (1987). *National trends in drug use and related factors among American high school students and young adults, 1975-1986.* Rockville, MD: U.S. Department of Health and Human Services.

National Institute on Drug Abuse. (1985). *Treatment services for adolescent substance abusers.* Rockville, MD: U.S. Department of Heath and Human Services.

Petersen, D.M. (1974). Some reflections on compulsory treatment of addiction. In J.A. Inciardi & C.D. Chambers (Eds.). *Drugs and the criminal justice system* (pp. 143-169). Beverly Hills: Sage.

Rosenberg, H., & Spiller, B. (1986). DUI offenders and mental health service providers: a shotgun marriage? In S.K. Valle (Ed.) *Drunk driving in America: Strategies and approaches to treatment*. NY: The Haworth Press.

Salmon, R. W. (1982). The role of coercion in rehabilitation of drug abusers. *Journal of Offender Counseling, Services & Rehabilitation, 6*(4), 59-70.

Saundra, T. (1988, May 15). Call to debate legalization of drugs becomes louder. *The Washington Post*, pp. A1, A20, A21.

Simpson, D.D. (1984). National treatment system evaluation based on the Drug Abuse Reporting Program (DARP) followup research. In National Institute on Drug Abuse. *Research Monograph 51: Drug abuse treatment evaluation: Strategies, progress, and prospects*. Rockville, MD. Author.

Singh, B.K., Joe, G.W., Lehman, W., Garland, J., & Sells, S.B. (1982). A descriptive overview of treatment modalities in federally funded drug abuse treatment programs. *The International Journal of the Addictions, 17*(6), 977-1000.

Steer, R.A. (1983). Retention in drug-free counseling. *The International Journal of the Addictions, 18*, 1109-1114.

Strug, E.L., & Hyman, M.M. (1981). Social networks of alcoholics. *Journal of Studies on Alcohol, 42*, 855-884.

System Sciences, (1978). *Final report: Evaluation of the treatment alternatives to street crime program, phase II*. Washington, DC: U.S. Government Printing Office.

Trice, H.M. & Beyer, J.M. (1982). Social control in worksettings: Using the constructive confrontation strategy with problem drinking employees. *Journal of Drug Issues, 12*, 21-49.

U.S. Department of Justice. (1983-a). *Prisoners and Alcohol*. Washington, DC: Author.

U.S. Department of Justice. (1983-b). *Prisoners and drugs*. Washington, DC: Author.

U.S. Department of Justice. (1979). *TASC: An approach for dealing with the substance abusing offender*. Washington, DC: U.S. Government Printing Office.

Ward, D. A. (1982). Introduction: Use of legal and non-legal coercion in the prevention and treatment of drug abuse. *Journal of Drug Issues, 12*, 1-4.

Ward, D.A. (1979). The use of legal coercion in the treatment of alcoholism: A methodological review. *Journal of Drug Issues, 9*, 387-398.

Weissman, J.C. (1979). Drug offender diversion: Philosophy and practices. *Drug Abuse and Alcoholism Review, 2*, 2-8.

Wish, E.D. (1987). *Drug use forecasting: New York 1984 to 1986*. Washington, DC: U.S. Department of Justice.

Alcohol Abuse and the Young Offender: Alcohol Education as an Alternative to Custodial Sentencing

Carol Greer
Alan Lawson
Steve Baldwin
Sandy Cochrane

SUMMARY. The exact nature of the relationship between alcohol abuse and offending remains unclear. The problem of how to address this relationship remains a matter of debate. The importance of dealing with this problem in the most effective way is highlighted by the need to maximise existing resources at a time of financial restraint. The goal is to design and implement interventions specific to the parameters of the problem—recognising the characteristics of the target population, and the demands of the judicial system.

Alcohol Education Courses (AECs) offer a range of techniques. From didactic information-based courses, through non-directive discussion courses, to behavioural skills packages, an attempt to intervene at a secondary level is made. The abusive alcohol consumption level of the population, or the problem of offending, or both, serve as that main targets of courses. If successful, these courses may offer a viable alternative to custodial sentencing, addressing the presenting problem directly. Evaluation of such services is crucial to their further implementation, with promising initial findings from controlled evaluation research.

The authors are members of the staff of the Department of Clincial Psychology at General Hospital in St. Helier, Jersey, the Channel Islands, United Kingdom, where Carol Greer is associated with the Charities Projects, Alan Lawson and Sandy Cochrane are associated with the Mathew Trust, and Steve Baldwin is associated with the Alcohol Education and Research Council.

Acknowledgement and thanks to Mrs. W. Janvrin-Tipping for the typing of this manuscript.

THE NATURE OF THE PROBLEM

The link between alcohol abuse and offending in the male population aged 16-29 has been established (Greenberg, 1981; Permanen, 1981; McGuire & Priestley, 1981). For this age group, 50% of all murders; 20% of all child abuse; 33% of all domestic violence involved alcohol abuse (Simms, 1988). In Scotland, during 1985, 78% of all assaults; 80% of all Breach of the Peace offences, and 88% of all Criminal Damage were drink-related (Baldwin et al., 1986).

While Britain has been 20th in the League Table of National Consumption of Alcohol/Person, (IAS 1988), with an average of 7.1 litres/person/year, some evidence has suggested a minority group aged 18-24 years, mainly male, exceeded "safe/sensible" alcohol consumption levels (i.e., over 21 units/week). This was directly related to the high levels of petty offences attributed to this age group (Rutherford, 1988). Lobbying by alcohol abuse agencies has led the British government to call for an answer to the problem: "Ministers must contend with the clear relationship between uncontrolled drinking and criminal activity" (Douglas Hurd, 1988).

THE MEDICALISATION OF ALCOHOL ABUSE AND OFFENDING

The range of alternatives to address the problems presented from alcohol abuse and offending has been limited (Greenberg, 1981). Between 55-85% of all cases within Scottish young offender institutions involved alcohol abuse (Baldwin et al., 1986). High levels of recidivism have suggested that custodial sentencing has failed to meet the needs of the judicial system, and not addressed the link between alcohol abuse and offending. Custodial sentencing has shown no effectiveness in reducing subsequent offending (Blackburn, 1980). Evidence from subsequent alcohol consumption levels, after release from institutions has been equivocal (Hershon, Cook and Foldes, 1974).

In the 1960s and 1970s, the medical/disease model of alcohol abuse predominated, leading to medical/psychiatric interventions (Gath et al., 1968). In the USA, alcohol abuse and subsequent offending has been answered by an expansion in psychiatric care interventions (Mitchell, 1971). For all these medical interventions, no systematic controlled evaluation of their effectiveness was completed (Miller and Hester, 1980). Total abstinence from alcohol consumption was the goal of most medically-directed interventions (Miller, 1984). By its design, the medical approach to alcohol abuse concentrated on alcohol consumption reduction, and eventual abstinence, with little attention to the variable of offending and reconviction. Some claims have been made for the efficacy of "dry interventions" (Elkins, 1980), and of detoxification (Rada & Kelner, 1979). No controlled systematic evaluation related to subsequent alcohol levels, and/or offending rates has been achieved, however.

Britain has been slow to adopt detoxification techniques for offending. The first provision of "wet shelters" was in Manchester and in Leeds (Ward, 1985). With problems of ease of access, and pressure to meet cost-effectiveness goals, assessment of such services was limited. Lack of clear definition of outcome measures has led to problems in interpretation of efficacy of services (i.e., does continued use of the detoxification centre indicate success or failure to help the individual reduce his/her problems?) (Orford, 1985).

In addition, support for the relevance of detoxification of young offenders with drink problems has been questioned.

Detoxification may be necessary for offenders with a high level of physiological dependence on alcohol, a condition not often found in young offenders (Orford, 1985; Ward, 1985). The movement away from detoxification as a medical panacea for all alcohol abuse reflects a movement towards a different conception of the problem of alcohol misuse.

THE DEMEDICALISATION OF ALCOHOL ABUSE

Interventions

From the late 1970s there has been more recognition of the inadequacy of the medical model to explain the relationship between alcohol abuse and offending. Theoretical constructs of the problem of alcohol misuse in young people have adopted ideas from Social

Learning Theory, with subsequent models focusing on learning of inappropriate behaviour and allied deficit/excesses of related skills (Orford, 1985).

This reconceptualisation has resulted in a need to redefine the parameters of the problem focusing on the characteristics of the target population, and the social, personal and environmental input to the problem. It has become clear that young people conceptualise alcohol misuse in a very different way from professionals involved in reducing alcohol misuse (Heather, 1982). Young people may have a higher tolerance for "alcohol abuse" than those who work in alcohol abuse. There is a reluctance to acknowledge that any problem exists, from those most at risk of self-abuse with alcohol.

Basic knowledge about alcohol consumption was limited within the 16-29 age group. In Greater London, 12% of young males surveyed drank each day—yet none of them knew the answers to more than 50% of an alcohol basic facts questionnaire (e.g., standard unit of alcohol?) (Alcohol Update, S.C.A. 1988).

This lack of basic knowledge about alcohol consumption and related inaccurate concepts of what constitutes alcohol abuse may have increased subsequent demand for interventions at a primary level (i.e., before alcohol problems begin), as opposed to secondary interventions, (i.e., once the alcohol problem has developed).

PRIMARY VERSUS SECONDARY INTERVENTIONS

Provision of large-scale alcohol education to present facts about what constitutes alcohol abuse and how it relates to offending may be the long-term answer, allied to clear directives on how to drink safely and sensibly (Alcohol Update, 1988). Individuals working in the alcohol field have suggested that tighter fiscal policy and increases in alcohol prices are required so that the most effective reductions in both alcohol abuse and related crime occurs (Kendall, 1983). The new EEC guidelines which tax alcohol (in operation by 1992), may increase alcohol consumption by 1/3, with a related increase in petty offences (Rutherford, 1988).

Currently, however, the situation is not open to implementation of tighter price control, despite evidence of its efficacy, via a decrease of 9% in all indices of alcohol-related crime (Smith, 1988).

In Scotland £3.5 million is spent on alcohol per day, with related criminal activity costing £15.79 million (Alcohol Concern, 1985).

Any primary intervention should be set in the context of the acceptability of alcohol consumption, and its attractiveness to young people. In the 1930s and 1940s, males aged 18-24 consumed the lowest amount of alcohol in the population. Targeting of this age group with the "Beer is Best" campaign increased their overall consumption. In the 1980s, the peak age for alcohol consumption is 20 years (Rutherford, 1988). Drink advertising directed at those in their twenties has been found to be the most attractive to people in their mid-late teens (Aitken, Leather and Scott, 1987). No clear evidence has suggested a causal relationship between alcohol and advertising. A *possible* link however, was strong enough for the Masham Report (1987) to promote a ban on cinema and television advertising of alcohol, with a request to television programmers to promote the negative side-effects of alcohol misuse.

SECONDARY INTERVENTIONS AND DEMEDICALISATION

While primary interventions/primary strategies may be the long-term goal of persons working in the alcohol field, young offenders with drink problems require specific interventions targeted directly at their problem. Costs incurred by society related to alcohol misuse and offending at £15.74 million have led to the design of effective secondary intervention procedures to target the link between drinking and offending (Alcohol Concern Factsheet, 1985).

The demedicalisation of alcohol abuse/offending relationship, and expansion of non-statutory agencies which offer services to the courts for young offenders (Robinson & Tether, 1983), has switched the focus from changing social systems towards change of the young offender (Staulcup et al., 1979). This has been consistent with Social Learning Theory, and a perceived need to re-educate young offenders about alcohol use and misuse (Williams et al., 1968).

Alcohol Education Courses (AECs) in a variety of forms were designed to direct the provision of information about alcohol misuse, and subsequently to introduce behavioural skills components.

The characteristics of the client population to be treated has been paramount in design of these packages. The age of regular alcohol consumption has been reduced (Aitken, 1978), with early high consumption of alcohol predictive of heavy consumption in the mid-twenties (Ghodsian and Power, 1987). Alcohol consumption above safe limits (i.e., more than 21 units/week) was seen by young people to offer positive benefits in self-confidence, reduction of boredom, sexual attractiveness and social popularity (Annis, 1985), with scant regard to negative costs from offending and conviction.

Early AECs were formed on the provision of information on alcohol use and misuse. These have been offered to young offenders, usually via probation orders from the courts. Courses usually involved less than 10 young offenders in groups, with the overall goal of either total abstention or controlled drinking (where the offender remained within safe limits). Efficacy of controlled drinking goals for young offenders has received strong support (Miller and Hester, 1980. Polich et al., 1981; Robertson and Heather, 1982). In addition, the benefits of short AECs, (i.e., 6 sessions of 2 hours), may be more effective than more lengthy AEC programmes (Miller, 1983).

Systematic evaluation of these services has failed to find support for the implementation of AECs, largely because controlled evaluation has not been integrated to their design or implementation (Bailey, 1966; Baldwin et al., 1986). Until the late 1960s, provision of information on alcohol misuse was believed to be sufficient to promote behavioural change (Williams et al., 1968). It was believed that by changing attitudes, change in alcohol consumption could be addressed (Goodstadt, 1978). No evidence however, has been found to support this. In fact, information provision may increase consumption (Kinder, Pape & Walfish, 1980).

Early information-based AECs did not collect evidence of reduced alcohol consumption. Absence of evidence about offending levels has also reflected ambiguity about efficacy of AEC provision (Bailey, 1966). Evidence on offending rate reductions was at best equivocal. It has been suggested that more problem-specific interventions should be designed (Spence, 1979). This was in contrast to predominant beliefs that most secondary interventions with young offenders do not affect either outcome variables of alcohol consumption or offending behaviour (Feldman, 1976). The full assessment of efficacy of any proposed AEC intervention (and the need for systematic evaluation) has not occurred, failing to answer the staff need for information about the outcomes, the needs of the clients, and the needs of the courts.

THE DEVELOPMENT OF ALCOHOL EDUCATION COURSES AS SECONDARY INTERVENTIONS

AECs were developed in England to provide viable alternatives to custodial sentencing, fines, deferred sentencing and cautioning. They have expanded in number over the past eight years; more than 471 AECs have been completed throughout England and Scotland (Cochrane et al., 1989).

English courses still have reflected the information-based origins of the early AECs. Courses have developed in Scotland since 1982, using a behavioural package. Introduction of behavioural components, such as drink diaries, self-monitoring and examination of clients' offending history, and training in alternative skills to reduce drinking behaviour, has now extended to England. A national survey revealed at least 60% (n = 31) of all reported AECs (n = 55) implemented behavioural designs. In total, more than 3409 individuals (mostly males) have completed an AEC since 1981 (Cochrane et al., 1989).

Expansion of these courses, with the ready adoption by statutory and non-statutory agencies, increases the potency of controlled evaluations as viable secondary intervention techniques. From 1976, approximately £1.5 million has been spent on their implementation (Cochrane et al., 1988). Eighty nine percent claimed some form of evaluation; half examined alcohol consumption levels and a third examined offending rates. None of these evaluations was controlled, however, and therefore interpretation of their findings has been limited.

Confounding variables, however, such as marital change, employment change, physical illness and financial reasons could not be excluded as factors in observed reductions in alcohol abuse and offending after attendance on an AEC (Saunders and Kershaw, 1979).

EVALUATION OF ALCOHOL EDUCATION COURSES

Lack of controlled evaluation data from English AECs has reduced the confidence of the courts and prospective clients in provision of Alcohol Education Courses. Trends which suggested the inadequacy of information-based alcohol education courses presented problems in justifying continuation of such services, and the subsequent proposed expansion of AECs to incorporate behavioural components (Hawkins, 1982). Validation of AECs via controlled evaluations was crucial in justifying extension of funding and staffing, and in boosting the morale of staff in statutory and non-statutory agencies responsible for administration of courses (Baldwin et al., 1987). A call for more controlled evaluations has coincided with increased AEC availability (Blackburn, 1980; Greenberg, 1981; and Pernanen, 1981; Vingilis, 1981).

Introduction of behavioural AECs has produced favourable conditions in England for both alcohol consumption reduction and for improvements in offending (Menary, 1986; Godfrey and Leahy, 1986). Controlled evaluations have still not occurred, possibly due to the ethical difficulties of selecting a control group who receive no interventions. In Scotland, however, conditions have allowed the first controlled evaluations of AEC effectiveness as a secondary intervention for both alcohol abuse and offending (Baldwin et al., 1989 a, b, c, d).

THE SCOTTISH EVALUATION RESEARCH

Individuals were referred from:

a. Dundee — Group 1 behavioural, or Group 2 talk based
b. Forfar — Group 1 information-based, or Group 2 no intervention control
c. Glasgow — Group 1 behavioural, or Group 2 talk-based
d. Noranside — Young offender institution — Group 1 behavioural, or Group 2 no intervention control.

Control groups were matched with course groups at all locations on all factors other than AEC type. Each course lasted 6 weeks, with 2 hour sessions. The behavioural course focussed on skill acquisition, drinking/offending analysis, and subsequent behavioural modification; talk based courses were non-didactic, non-directive group discussions of alcohol abuse and subsequent offending. Information-based courses focussed on provision of information on alcohol consumption. Control groups were offered no interventions.

The conclusion was that both talk-based courses and information-based courses reduced alcohol consumption. The behavioural courses however achieved significant reductions compared with a control group. The behavioural course was also successful in significant reduction in conviction rates and self-reported offending when compared to a control group, in a young offenders institution. All clients who had attended any form of AEC reported ideal drinking levels (i.e., consumption of alcohol they wished to achieve) within safe drinking limits. This was reflected in an increase in confidence ratings in their ability to achieve their targets (Baldwin et al., 1988 a, b, c, d).

Follow-up interviews were conducted at approximately 12 months after each course, with an overall follow-up rate of 70%. On the two major dependent variables (alcohol consumption and conviction rate/self reported offending), the behavioural course significantly reduced both variables; the other courses both reduced alcohol consumption, but not subsequent offending rates. Most individuals who had been on courses reported changes in their ideal drinking target within safe limits guidelines (i.e., the ideal consumption level), with a related increase in confidence in achieving this target.

The Scottish research produced the conclusion that behavioural AECs in an institution significantly reduced levels of alcohol abuse and offending. It also demonstrated the need for controlled evaluations as an integral part of implementation of successful secondary interventions.

The importance of the clarity of the findings is threefold. First, for clients referred to courses, they may be more than an "easy option," as they have been seen by some within the judicial system (Hawkins, 1982). In addition, the specificity of the design allows direct focus on the problems that first brings the client into the system. Debate has focused on voluntary attendance versus attendance on a condition of probation, or as part of a deferred sentence. Volunteering has been seen as preferential over coercion (McLoone, Oulds and Harris, 1987). Demonstration of AEC efficacy may promote willingness of clients to enter the course. There is insufficient evidence however to warrant removal of deferred sentencing/probation orders.

Second, the efficacy of AECs for statutory agency/non-statutory agency staff who implement the courses may aid the promotion of the courses to clients. Problems in morale, funding and staffing levels (Baldwin & Heather, 1987) have made implementation of such secondary intervention measures difficult. Calls for increased liaison between agencies offering such services should be addressed (Godfrey & Leahy, 1986). In Tyne Tees, operation of workshops to increase staff morale by promotion of the efficacy of their role has been effective.

Finally, benefits from systematic controlled evaluations should be demonstrated to the judiciary and administrative staff. Information about the benefit of such courses when making referrals may stimulate course attendance, or further referrals. Referrals have been problematic in previous assessments of course effectiveness (Baldwin, Cuthbert, Greer and McCluskey, 1988). Court officials and administrative staff have faced conflicts between the need to punish individuals for their offences and the desire to rehabilitate the offender. Alcohol Education Courses, by addressing the problem of alcohol abuse and offending, can meet the challenge of reduction in alcohol consumption and offending/conviction rates. While not a panacea for all individuals, or all levels of abuse, evaluation data can justify the continued claim of AECs on staff time and resources.

AECs OR SELF-HELP MANUALS?

The problem of limited resources and staff has produced a move to promote the most effective form of secondary intervention for the interface between alcohol abuse and offending. While group-based AEC packages have grown in popularity, a move towards use of self-help manuals promoting information on alcohol consumption has occurred. These manuals range from information provision about alcohol, to the promotion of anti-offending skill acquisition (McMurran & Boyle, 1989). Rigorous evaluation has not been incorporated in these studies, however, reducing accurate assessment of effectiveness. Self-administered "minimal interventions" have become more popular (Daw 1982), despite lack of systematic evaluation.

A recent study within a penal institution of use of self-help manuals compared with group-based interventions using the same manual found little support for either form of minimal intervention for reductions either in alcohol abuse or offending (McMurran & Boyle, 1989). Clients were randomly selected (with no regard to prior levels of alcohol abuse), confounding result interpretation, however.

Earlier studies have found support for the use of self-help manuals both for individuals and as group-based interventions (Miller and Taylor, 1980). Clients given a self-help manual and self-monitoring card were equally successful in alcohol reduction, compared with subjects offered 10 sessions with an alcohol abuse therapist (Miller & Taylor, 1980). The cost-effective benefits of self-help manuals compared to AECs may lead to rapid adoption of these, as successful minimal interventions for young offenders with drink problems. More work is required however on the types of clients for whom the manuals may be suitable, with proper controlled evaluation of their effects, before general adoption is achieved. When a behavioural self-control package was introduced in groups (or as a manual for individuals), no significant differences between interventions were reported in reducing alcohol consumption (Miller, 1980). All measures were equally successful, which supported the cost-effectiveness value of the manual (Skutle and Berge, 1987).

CONCLUSION

Research on the efficacy on self-help manuals, both in individual or group-based administrations, is required. Use of one form of secondary intervention need not exclude others, and they may exist in a complementary relationship, answering the needs of different clients. Until controlled evaluations have been achieved, however, this cannot be resolved.

Effective secondary intervention strategies are required to address relationships between alcohol abuse and offending. Measures to operate at a primary level may be the long-term answer, with tighter policy controls. Secondly, interventions should be designed with the specified characteristics of the target population, and clear and distinct goals, relevant to the needs of users of the service. Only via controlled evaluations can effectiveness questions be answered.

REFERENCES

Aitken, P.P., Leathar, D.S. & Scott, A.C. "Ten to Sixteen Year Olds Perception of Advertisements for Alcoholic Drinks." A.R.U. Department of Marketing. Strathclyde University, Glasgow.

Bailey, W.C. (1966). Correctional Outcome: An evaluation of 100 reports. The Journal of Criminal Law, Criminology and Political Science, 57, (2), 153-160.

Baldwin, S., & Heather, N. (1987). Alcohol Education Courses and Offenders: Survey of U.K. Agencies. Alcohol and Alcoholism. Vol. (22) No. 1, pp. 79-82.

Baldwin, S., Greer, C., & Cochrane, S., Therapeutic Outcomes for Individuals Court Ordered for Intervention of Alcohol Problems, (In press).

Baldwin, Ford, I., Heather, N., (1987). Drink and Crime No 1 Community Care, April (2), pp. 12-13.

Baldwin, S., Braggins, F., Ford, I., & Heather, N. (1987). Drink and Crime No 2 Community Care, April 9, pp. 22-23.

Baldwin, Cuthbert, J., Greer, C., & McCluskey, S. (1988). Effectiveness of an Alcohol Education Course for Young Offenders in Urban Courts. (In Preparation).

Baldwin, Braggins, Carnegie, E., Lawson, A., Masters, G. & Mooney, J. (1988). Comparison of Alcohol Education Courses, their Effectiveness in Urban and Rural Settings. (In Preparation).

Balfour-Sclare, A. (1985). Treatment of alcoholism in Scotland. International Journal of Offender Therapy and Comparitive Criminology. pp. 153-165.

Blackburn, R. (1980). Still not Working? A Look at Recent Outcomes in Offender Rehabilitation. (Paper presented at Scottish B.P.S. Conference on Deviance.) University of Sterling. Brewers Society Statistical Handbook (1986).

Cochrane, Baldwin, Greer, C. & McCluskey, S. (1988). Alcohol Education Courses and Offenders: Update of U.K. Services. Alcohol and alcoholism. (In Press).

Doherty, F. & Davies, J.D. (1987). "Life Events and Addiction: A Critical Review." British Journal of Addiction. 82: pp. 127-137.

Dow, M.G.T. (1982). Behavioural Bibliotherapy: Theoretical and Methodological Issues in Outcome Research into Self-Help Programmes. In Main, C.J.

(ed). Clinical Psychology and Medicine: A Behavioural Perspective. New York, Plenum Press. pp. 177-204.

Elkins, R.L. "Concept Sensitization. Treatment of Alcoholism: Contributions of successful conditioning to subsequent abstinence maintainance." Addictive Behaviours, 1980, (5), pp. 67-89.

Engs, R.C. (1982). "Let's look before we leap: the cognitive and behavioural evaluation of a University alcohol education programme. pp. 39-49.

Feldman, M.P. (1976). Criminal behaviour. London. Wiley Press.

Ghodsian, M. & Power, C. Alcohol Consumption between the ages of Sixteen and Twenty-three in Britain: A longitudinal study. British Journal of Addiction. (1987) 82, pp. 175-180.

Godfrey, R., Leahy, N. (1986). Education with the Probation Service. Alcohol Concern, March 2 (8), pp. 17-19.

Goodstadt, M.S., (1978). Alcohol and Drug Education: Models and Outcomes. Health Education Monographs, Fall, 260-279.

Grant, M. (1982). Alcohol Education: Does it really effect drinking problems? Journal of the Royal Society of Health, 102, 5, pp. 201-204.

Greenberg, S.W. (1981). Alcohol and Crime: A methodological critique of the literature. In J.J. Collins (ed). Drinking and Crime. New York. Guilford Press.

Hamilton, J.R. (1976). Helping the Drunken Offender. Health and Social Service Journal, August 28, pp. 1550-1551.

Hawkins, R.O. (1982). Adolescent Alcohol Abuse: A Review. Developmental and Behavioural Paediatrics, 3 (2), June 83-87.

Heather, N. (1981). Relationships between Delinquency and Drunkenness among Scottish Young Offenders. British Journal on Alcohol and Alcoholism, 16 (2), pp. 145-153.

Heather, N. (1982). An Alcohol Dependence and Problem Drinking in Scottish Young Offenders. British Journal on Alcohol and Alcoholism, 17 (4), pp. 145-153.

Heather, N., Robertson, I. (1983). Controlled Drinking (second edition) Methuen. London.

Hershon, H.I., Cook, T. & Foldes, P.A. (1974). What Shall we do with the Drunker Offender?, British Journal of Psychiatry, 124, pp. 327-335.

Kendell, R. The Beneficial Consequences of the United Kingdom's Declining Per Capita Consumption of Alcohol in 1979-1982. Alcohol and Alcoholism, 19, 4, pp. 271-276, 1984.

Light, R. (1986). The Habitual Drunken Offender. Alcohol Concern Fact-sheet.

Maynard, A. Alcohol Research Fact-sheet, September 1985. Alcohol Concern. Centre for Health Economics, York University.

Maguire and Priestley. (1985). Offending Behaviour: Skills and Strategems for Going Straight. Batsford Press.

McLoone, P., Oulds, G. & Morris, J. (1987). Alcohol Education Groups: Compulsion & Voluntarism. Probation, 25.

McMurran, M., Boyle, M. Evaluation of Self-help Manual for Young Offenders Who Drink. (In preparation).

Miller, W.R. Treating Problem Drinkers: What works? Behaviour Therapy, Volume 5. No. 1. pp. 15-18, 1980.

Miller, W.R. (1987). Techniques to modify hazardous drinking patterns. Behaviour Therapy (25) pp. 425-438.

Miller, W.R., & Baca, L.M. (1983). Two year follow-up of bibliotherapy and therapist directed controlled drinking. Behaviour Therapy (14): pp. 441-448.

Miller, W.R. & Munoz, R.F. How to control your drinking. Albuquerque. University of New Mexico Press. 1976.

Miller, W.R. & Taylor, C. Relative Effectiveness of Bibliotherapy, Individual and Group Self-control Training in Treatment of Problem Drinkers. Addictive Behaviours. 5. pp. 13-24, 1980.

Miller, W.R. & Hester, R.K. "Treating the Problem Drinker: Modern Approaches" in W.R. Miller (ed). The Addictive Behaviours: Treatment of Alcoholism, Drug Abuse, Smoking and Obesity. New York: Pergamon Press. 1980.

Orford, J. (1985). Problem Drinking: A Psychological Perspective. Wiley Press.

Pernanen, K. (1981). Theoretical Aspects of the Relationship between Alcohol Use and Crime, in J.J. Collins (editor) Drinking and Crime. New York. Guilford Press.

Polich, J.M., Armor, D.J. & Braiker, H.B. The Course of Alcoholism Four Years After Treatment. New York. Wiley. 1981.

Rada, R.T. & Kellner, R. (1979). "Drug Treatment in Alcoholism." In I. Davies and D.J. Greenblat (Eds). Recent Developments in Psychopharmacology. New York. Grune and Stratton.

Robertson, I., Heather, N. (1982). An Alcohol Education Course with Young Offenders: A Preliminary Report. Alcohol and Alcoholism.

Robertson, I., Heather, N., Dzialdowski, A., Crawford, J., & Winton, M., A Comparison of Minimal versus Intensive Controlled Drinking Treatment Interventions for Problem Drinkers. British Journal of Clinical Psychology (1986), 25, pp. 185-194.

Robinson, D., Tether, P. (1985). Preventing Alcohol Problems: A Guide to Local Action. Tavistok, London. 1986.

Rutherford, D. (1988). Drink Related Offending in Young People. Institute of Alcohol Studies.

Saunders, B. Alcohol: The Prevention Paradoxes. Presented to the British Association for the Advancement of Science Symposium, at the University of Strathclyde, Scotland, August 1985.

Saunders, W.M. & Kershaw, P.W. (1979). Spontaneous Remission from Alcoholism: A Community Study. British Journal of Addiction, 74, pp. 251-265.

Skutle, A., & Berg, G. (1987). "Training in Controlled Drinking for Early Stage Problem Drinkers". British Journal of Addiction, 82, pp. 331-342.

Spence, S. (1979). Social Skills Training with Adolescent Male Offenders – No 1: Short-term effects. Behaviour Research and Therapy 117, pp. 7-16.

Spence, S. (1981). Social Skills Training with Adolescent Male Offenders: No 2:

Short-term, long-term and generalised effects. Behavioural Psychotherapy, 19, pp. 349-368.

Smith, R. (1987). Action on alcohol at last. British Medical Journal. (vd. 295, 26th Sept. 1987) p. 740.

Vingilis, E. (1981). A literature review of the young drinking offender. Is he a problem drinker? British Journal of Addiction, 76, pp. 27-46.

Ward, T. (1985). "Not so simple drunkenness." Alcohol Concern Fact-sheet, pp. 14-15.

Williams, A.F., Di Cicco, L.M. & Unterberger, H. (1969). Philosophy and evaluation of an Alcohol Education Programme. Quarterly Journal of Studies on Alcohol, 29, pp. 685-702.

The Convergence
of the Mentally Disordered
and the Jail Population

William H. Snow
Katharine Hooper Briar

SUMMARY. This paper addresses the prevalence and implications of the mentally ill, developmentally disabled, substance abuser, and other mentally impaired offenders in the jail system. Drawing on data from a jail's central intake screening system, the authors argue for more systematic attention by service providers in the community and criminal justice personnel to the disabling conditions that may precipitate and reinforce criminal behavior. Differential responses to these special needs or "pseudo-offenders" are recommended.

Jails serve as modern day asylums, housing the mentally ill, public inebriates, drug addicts, developmentally disabled and people with various medical problems (Briar, 1983; Collins & Deviny, Notes 1 and 2). The general public tends to regard these individuals as deviant since they exhibit non-conforming behaviors and sometimes commit crimes. Such individuals constitute a significant portion of the criminal justice population. These special needs offenders might be more appropriately termed "pseudo-offenders." Their disabling conditions in some way contribute to their criminal behavior, either precipitating or reinforcing its likelihood. Moreover, in-

William H. Snow, PhD, is Assistant Professor of Psychology at Bethany College.

Katharine Hooper Briar, DSW, is Associate Professor of Social Work at the University of Washington.

This research is based in part on a grant from the National Institute of Corrections.

dividual deviance does not end with arrest and incarceration; this population takes their problems with them to jail. As they contend with often intolerable conditions and go without therapeutic attention, jail aggravates their problems. Neither cell mates nor jail personnel are well equipped to deal with crises caused by drug and alcohol withdrawal, suicidal episodes, interpersonal aggression, psychotic behavior or epileptic seizures.

Little studied and largely forgotten, this population receives scant attention from policymakers and social reform advocates. Were more information about them available, their needs might be better addressed. This paper examines the prevalence and characteristics of a sample of mentally disordered inmates in a Pacific Northwest county-city jail. Findings suggest major changes—both in the community and in the criminal justice system.

This inquiry focuses on the prevalence of mental illness, substance abuse, developmental disabilities, and medical problems affecting judgment. The scope of the inquiry is limited, but it is hoped it will prompt more inclusive analyses of other contributors and determinants of criminal behavior. More systematic examination of the precipitants and reinforcers of criminal offenses may eventually compel the development of management and disposition options more relevant to the presenting problems of incarcerated persons.

JAILS: ENDANGERING ENVIRONMENTS

The problems of special needs offenders can best be underscored by first examining the general characteristics of U.S. jails. The overcrowded and unsanitary conditions of jails pose major problems for both the jailers and jailed alike. Despite law suits, jail closures and attempts to enforce improved physical standards, substandard conditions persist. Few of the estimated 4000-6000 jail facilities have sought and met jail accreditation guidelines; moreover, an insignificant number have complied with the American Medical Association standards for health care (Ford & Kerle, 1981). Of those jails that meet standards for ventilation, sanitation, fire safety, recreation and nutrition, few address the treatment requirements of special needs offenders. Clearly, anyone who is arrested and incarcerated will experience stress. However, little is known about its effects on the mental and physical health of inmates (Owens, 1980). Even less is known about the consequences of jail incarceration on mentally disordered inmates. Symptoms are aggravated by jail conditions and service deficits as reflected by jail suicide statistics: 85% of all jail suicides occur among intoxicated inmates within the first 12 hours of incarceration (Hudson & Butts, 1979; Coalition for National Jail Reform). Other statistics characterize typical suicide victims as white males, 22 to 27 years of age with a history of alcohol and drug use. Approximately 75% had made past attempts. Despite such histories, records show jail personnel officials rarely identify these inmates as high risk (Deheer & Schweitzer, 1985).

Looking at the situation from the other side of the bars, jailers perceive disturbed and disabled inmates as threatening their own physical safety. They argue that troubled inmates are often perpetrators or victims of sexual and physical assaults, and they have particular trouble managing and confining unmedicated, psychotic inmates, sometimes with tragic results. For example, a jailer in one local jail used a choke hold to restrain the violent episode of a psychotic inmate. Believing he was both protecting his own life and that of the inmate, the jailer, in his attempts to restrain the disabled man, fatally suffocated him (Jail death, 1980).

Certainly, jailers know that any inmate is a potential threat to the lives of everyone in the jail. Fire, disease, contamination and other calamities are real concerns. An inmate, caged, worried and abhorring the prolonged "dead time" that accompanies incarceration, might be pressed into desperate acting out behavior. Such desperation may be exacerbated by drug states, alcohol intoxication or psychosis. Considering that for some the average jail stay lasts over 10 weeks, one can see the intensifying effect of inadequate therapeutic attention and inadequate food, recreation and sanitation (Kurtz, 1981). One disturbed inmate set his clothes and bed on fire, threatening his own life and all the rest in the jail.

Jails have increasingly become public dumping grounds (Briar, 1983). Deinstitutionalized populations, unable to acquire care elsewhere, have become chronic segments of jail populations. Prison overcrowding has also forced surplus populations on jails. In 1978, one out of every 19 jail inmates was being held there due to state and federal prison overcrowding (Whitmer, 1980). As unemployment persists and rises, and cutbacks continue in publicly funded community social services, jails will absorb greater numbers of persons rejected by the community. With funding for jail alternatives eroded, institutions for many mentally and physically disabled no longer accessible, and community based support services stripped back, jails have the dubious distinction of being the one local institution where people will not be turned away.

With the influx of deinstitutionalized persons, jail personnel are forced to guard against discrimination, treating disabilities as presenting problems when they are not and failing to hold disabled persons responsible for their actions (Gibbons, Sawin & Gibbons, 1979). "Normalization" principles undergirding deinstitutionalization suggest that persons with disabilities be integrated in the community and treated as normally as possible, including prosecution for criminal behavior if warranted. While disabled offenders should not be absolved of their actions, as with all inmates, they do not surrender all rights to safe, appropriate care once incarcerated. Yet lawsuits against jails because of death, physical and mental damage serve to indicate that not all inmates are being cared for and managed adequately. Needed is increased sensitivity of jail personnel to the differential treatment and management needs of diverse populations, especially inmates with disabling conditions.

IDENTIFYING THE MENTALLY DISORDERED OFFENDER

To examine the prevalence and characteristics of the mentally disordered offenders in the jail, an exploratory research probe was undertaken in a Pacific Northwest urban jail. This jail houses a daily average of 280 men and women and annually books about 19,000. The data base from which the sample was identified consisted of case records from the Central Intake and Screening Program. A total of 1565 case records based on interviews with inmates were examined. These contained systematically collected information about mental and physical functioning, prior treatment and other information related to potential inmate problems in the jail. Early detection of presenting problems help jail staff classify inmates for housing and social service needs, as well as identify those eligible for jail or court release. Potential management problems created by a disabling condition necessitate that jailers and social service staff recognize the "special needs" status of an inmate.

Although jail screeners were trained and skilled in the assessment of impairment, interjudge reliability was not sought in the assessment process or in the assignment of cases into a mentally disordered offender typology. Thus, research findings cannot claim strong reliability. However, explicit criteria were used to assign cases.

Assessment was based upon clinical observation and history taking through inmate disclosure rather than the administration of psychological tests. Of the 1565 cases, 332 or 21% had been designated as mentally disordered. Among this subgroup, 74.3% were identified as substance abusers, 36.7% were mentally ill, 3.9% were developmentally or physically disabled and 14.5% were both mentally ill and substance abusing. These findings are not inconsistent with the 19 studies reviewed by Bentz and Noel (1983).

DEMOGRAPHIC ATTRIBUTES OF THE MENTALLY DISORDERED

The study sample generally reflected national trends in attributes of jail populations. For example, gender breakdowns were similar, with 87% of the inmates being male. Inmates were also economically marginal, with 65% of the sample reporting total assets of less than $1,000 (U.S. Dept. of Justice, 1980). The remainder had assets of less than $5,000. Only a few were homeowners.

Exceeding national trends for jail inmates, unemployment rates for this sample were 64%, compared to 40% nationally. Another difference was that the individuals in this study had more education as reflected in the national figures: 60.8% of the sample had at least 12 years of school and 18.9% had some college. Although black jail inmates comprise about 40% of the jail population nationally and over 35% of the local jail population, among those evaluated as having a mental disorder they constituted only 10% (U.S. Dept. of Justice, 1980). This finding suggests that judgments regarding troubled or bizarre behavior may be culturally bound. For example, problem behaviors of black inmates may be judged to be criminal rather than impairments caused by a mental disorder or substance abuse. It has been observed that black inmates are handled differently from their Caucasian counterparts in the criminal justice system. Piliavin and Briar (1964) found stereotyping among police officers to result in black youth being more frequently interrogated than white youths, even though officers lack evidence that a crime had been committed. Moreover, their research showed that black youth were given more severe dispositions than their white counterparts for similar violations. In this case, it is possible that blacks were reluctant to disclose their mental health or substance abuse problems.

Finally, 76% of the mentally disordered population had prior criminal records, a figure higher than that of the general population; 72.6% were being charged with a misdemeanor and 25.5% with a felony.

SUBSTANCE ABUSE

Substance abusers develop unnatural physiological states by ingesting or injecting drugs. Although they seem to have some control over their disability, their addiction reduces self-control. Some individuals, such as those using PCP, may exhibit violent criminal behavior while in a drug-induced state. Others, with costly habits to support may resort to crime to maintain their drug dependency.

Substance abusers were the most frequently represented category in the sample of mentally disordered inmates. Of the 74% who indicated such problems consisting of 15.7% of the total screened, 42% abused alcohol, 22% abused drugs and 36% abused both. Sixty-five percent claimed their substance abuse had persisted for over a year, and some of these admitted chronic problems of up to eight years. Given the prevalence of drug and alcohol abuse among these inmates, it is curious that only 10% were in treatment at the time of their arrest. Twenty-three percent indicated they had had prior treatment; 77% had been arrested before, and of these 82% had been arrested for misdemeanors. Clearly, despite laws which promote noncriminal treatment for some alcohol abusers through detoxification programs, this population still finds its way into the jail and criminal justice system. Annually, one of every three arrests made is for public intoxication (Coalition for National Jail Reform).

Substance abusers such as those using PCP often require physical constraint, the drugs and their effects causing extreme management problems for jail staff. Episodic behaviors including violence and mutilation especially tax the management skills of staff. But most jail facilities lack detoxification and mental health units. Such deficits in care increase the risk to substance abusers who experience life-threatening events such as withdrawal and suicidal impulses.

MENTAL ILLNESS

Mental illness is a broad term that encompasses a number of disturbed, behavioral and delusional states. Causation can not be determined in all cases but it is believed that some are organically based while others are due to extreme external stressors. Whatever the cause, the result is an individual who makes decisions based upon a distorted sense of reality.

The mentally ill comprised the second largest category in the study—36.7% of the sample. Sixty-three percent of these individuals had received treatment in the past; 23% were receiving services at the time of their arrest. Fifty percent had been charged with felonies.

This subgroup constituted 7.7% of the total bookings screened, a figure which may be compared with the estimated 10-20% (both mentally ill and retarded) promulgated by the National Jail Reform Coalition (National Coalition, Note 3). Systematic diagnosis using psychological tests would likely reveal higher rates of mental retardation and related mental health problems as found in a study of penitentiary inmates: in that study, 26.5% of the prisoners were diagnosed as having one mental disorder, 3.8% as having two or more (Jones, 1976).

Abramson, concerned over the "criminalization of mentally disordered behavior," argues that because of restriction in involuntary treatment, the mentally ill are increasingly being arrested and prosecuted. He notes that because of questions over their competence to stand trial, a number are shuffled back and forth between the jail and mental hospital (Abramson, 1976).

The cage-like structures of jails impede the effective care of mentally ill persons. Environmental and service deficits accelerate the disorientation and decompensation of such inmates and result in unmeasurable human costs for the victim and severe management problems for the jail. One mentally ill inmate not only set himself and his bedding on fire but also smashed his knuckles repeatedly against the cell bars. To prevent further injury and fire-setting he was moved to the sallyport, a connecting gateway to the cells. This exposed area, never intended for habitation, was the only section of the jail in which he could be continually monitored. In short, the mentally ill are not prepared to cope with jail life and jails are not prepared to cope with the mentally ill. Punishing their bizarre behavior with segregation or suspended privileges only increases their fear and suspicion. Suicide is one result.

When incarcerated, the mentally ill do not understand their rights, they may not know how to secure adequate counsel, and may have difficulty in communicating with their attorney and aiding in their own defense. One individual was discovered in a local jail facility who had been there over a month without action being taken. Previously institutionalized, she had been jailed for a misdemeanor and, being somewhat withdrawn, she had not asked for help or attention. Staff assumed she was in contact with her attorney and other proper authorities; in reality, no one was handling her case (Woman lost, 1980).

MENTAL ILLNESS AND SUBSTANCE ABUSE

Some mentally ill inmates are also substance abusers. They comprise 14.5% of the sample of mentally disordered inmates. Which condition preceded or reinforced the other varied; for some, use and abuse of substances like alcohol or drugs were a form of self-medication. Certainly, the depressive, manic, euphoric, and psychotic states that accompany abuse of these substances can be confused with mental disorders. For others, substance abuse created a mental health problem evident at booking. Either case demands appropriate assessment, therapeutic care and monitoring. Yet, since jails usually lack comprehensive drug, alcohol and mental health services and treatment facilities, jailers are forced to use physical force to control the troublesome and life-threatening behaviors of these inmates.

DEVELOPMENTAL AND PHYSICAL DISABILITIES

Only 3.9% of the study sample and less than 1% of the jail population could be identified as mentally retarded or developmentally disabled. In contrast, national figures range from a low of 5% to a high of 30% (Santamour & West, 1982). The low rate generated in the screening process can be attributed to the complexity of detection, a problem that has implications for all criminal justice personnel (Steinbock, 1976).

Detection is essential in reducing the recidivism among such persons, estimated to be three times that of other inmates (Schwartz, 1982). Within the criminal justice system, offenders with mental retardation are at a distinct disadvantage. They have a difficult time understanding their rights and they tend to confess overly quickly and make decisions without counsel (Bush, 1976). Proper assessment at intake is needed to identify individuals with special needs and to locate resources for habilitation, rehabilitation, and diversion programs (Santamour, 1986).

Finally, several inmates had mental disorders which resulted in part from a physical illness or disability. One individual's psychotic behaviors were suspected to have resulted from a brain tumor; another had been experiencing extreme depression due to hypoglycemia. Screeners were not trained to provide medical screening; thus the actual figure may have been much higher.

ALTERNATIVE PATHWAYS OF CARE?

The presence of developmentally disabled and other special needs offenders in the criminal justice system is a stark indication of the unintended consequences of deinstitutionalization and of cutbacks in community services. The presumed deviant, who once may have been treated in an institution, now faces a high risk of substituting one institutional experience for another. Unfortunately, the new system is at best indifferent to the special needs of such individuals. While it is true that some communities and jails have established diversion projects, most have not. Providing appropriate care to special needs offenders remains an overwhelming problem. For example, Whitmer reported a segment of the deinstitutionalized population in California who, despite outpatient community services, rotated in and out of jail (Whitmer, 1980). Some were too impaired to follow through on treatment plans; others failed even to initiate requests for service. Once in the criminal justice system, their impaired functioning — in many instances partially and in some instances completely treatable — became secondary to their offense.

As deinstitutionalization continues, jails will receive more developmentally disabled and mentally ill inmates. Citing his experience in California, Whitmer reported an example of a woman who earned the wrath of her neighbors (Whitmer, 1980). She tampered with their mail by day and cut their shrubbery by night. When she refused medication and it was learned that by legal standards she could not be involuntarily hospitalized, the neighbors referred their case to the district attorney and she was arrested.

Some populations end up in jail because of their inability to effectively use traditional outpatient care. A study of one deinstitutionalized psychiatric unit showed that 40% of its patients contacted a community agency, but that these contacts were infrequent and sporadic. Only 6% of the ex-patients were involved in ongoing outpatient treatment (Whitmer, 1980).

Too few pathways of care for persons with disabilities means that jails fill the gap in custodial care and services. On one hand, the presence of pseudo-offenders in the criminal justice system is a social indicator of the need for service innovations to more appropriately aid such persons. On the other hand, the pseudo-offender population signals a need for jail and prison based treatment services and facilities. But, given the impoverished state of funding to upgrade jail facilities to even minimal physical standards, such services and facilities might be seen as non-essential. Furthermore, the community social service network is stressed not just by the deinstitutionalized populations but by funding cutbacks. Limited in its resources, the community social service network cannot undertake the intensive outreach, tracking and monitoring that might steer some pseudo-offenders toward alternative pathways of care.

BARRIERS TO NORMALIZATION

Compounding the effects of inadequate community based services is the tendency of pseudo-offenders to be ostracized because of their disability and lack of conformity. The slurred speech of a developmentally disabled adult or the eccentric behaviors of a mentally ill person encourages communities to label them deviant. Labeling and rejection increase marginality and the likelihood that they are headed for jail. The inaccessibility of alternative institutional care hastens the community reject along this path.

Certain variables help determine community acceptance; these variables resemble those used to determine whether a person can be released from police custody or from jail while awaiting trial. A review of these variables helps to explain the prevalence of these disabled persons in jails. According to Wiseman (1971), five major factors account for community acceptance or rejection. The first factor involves exhibiting proper social graces and behavior, including dress and demeanor, as well as conduct in stores, schools, restaurants and other public places. An individual must be able to appear in public without attracting undue negative attention. Many mentally ill, developmentally and sometimes physically disabled, as well as substance abusing individuals do not meet this standard. The second major factor needed for community acceptance is employment. Success in the workplace has always tended to be an indicator of individual worth; the unemployed are blamed for their lack of industriousness and motivation. Because finding a job requires "selling" oneself to the employer, recently deinstitutionalized persons who lack training in the desired behaviors have problems finding work. The developmentally disabled especially suffer. Unable to compete with higher functioning individuals they are often relegated to sheltered workshops or simple menial tasks, if employed at all.

The third critical factor for community acceptance involves residing at a good address. But community residents hearing of proposed group homes for their area express fears of lowered property values and threats to personal safety (Tacoma News Tribune, 1982). Since higher level socioeconomic communities resist having such establishments in their neighborhoods, group homes and half way houses are usually relegated to low income areas. Individuals not living in group homes but residing alone face similar problems. Economically disadvantaged, they must reside in impoverished areas with lower rents but also lower housing standards and higher crime rates.

The fourth criterion for community acceptance involves having socially acceptable companions. Yet companions may be themselves troubled and deviant. Lacking access to the workplace and "upstanding" neighborhoods, these individuals draw their companions from their impoverished surroundings. Finally, people need a good personal history and biography for acceptability. This factor is often contingent upon successful compliance with the other four criteria; a poor work record, criminal convictions, drug abuse, and mental illness do not constitute a "good personal history."

Not only do the disabilities, lifestyle and absence of treatment which affect this marginal population increase the likelihood of incarceration, but these characteristics also increase the chance that if arrested they will remain in custody and then in jail for some time. This potentiality becomes evident in the comparison of community acceptability criteria proposed by Wiseman (1971) with jail criteria for release on personal recognizance (Release criteria, Note 4):

Police Custody and *Jail Release Criteria* vs.	*Community Qualifications*
1. Officer discretion	1. Knowing the proper social graces and behavior
2. Employment	2. Employment
3. Community ties	3. Location of a good address
4. Proper identification	4. Acceptable companions
5. No similar offenses No felonies No failures to appear in court	5. Good personal history and biography

Release criteria differentially affect the mentally disordered since their rate of unemployment is over 50% higher than that of general jail inmate populations. Joblessness and impoverishment also affect whether they will be able to use bail as a means of release (Miller, 1978). In addition, release based on a prior record hampers pseudo-offenders, since 76% had prior records. And, although police and jail managers use their own discretion in release decisions, offenders must have met the other criteria to warrant consideration. It seems likely that police officers and jail managers are not eager to release a disabled offender whose behavior continues to be deviant and unpredictable.

As noted earlier, little is known about the adaptation of disabled persons to jails and prisons. In certain cases, persons with histories of prior institutional care may actually prefer jail or prison life to life in the community. Such accommodations may also reinforce criminal behavior. For example, one developmentally disabled man was sent to prison for stealing a red truck. When he was finally released, his anxiety led him to seek reincarceration. Using his impaired reasoning, he looked for another red truck to steal; he knew no other way to return to jail, and he thought the truck had to be red (Hinkle, Note 5). Thus, incarceration may thwart any independent living skills a disabled person has been helped to acquire in group care facilities or outpatient skill oriented treatment programs. Mutual rejection—the community's rejecting the disabled person and the disabled person's rejecting the community—may be reinforced by incarceration.

IMPLICATIONS FOR INTERVENTION

The jail functions as an alternative form of institutional care for mentally disturbed, impaired and others whose deviant mental behaviors violate community norms. As such it offers a strategic base to systematically divert them to more appropriate social care arrangements. Central intake and screening programs, established in a few jails, must be developed to facilitate such a process. Public concern for some of the unintended negative consequences of deinstitutionalization cannot be registered until data about the prevalence of these "pseudo-offenders" are routinely promulgated. Community advocates may be able to ally themselves more closely with jail personnel in attempts to educate as well as to intervene on behalf of disturbed and disabled persons.

As detection improves and diagnostic and screening services become more sophisticated, the basis on which persons are considered pseudo-offenders may expand to include others whose crimes cloak some of their precipitating problems. The unemployed are but one example of such a population; their precipitating offense may be linked to the desperation of prolonged improvishment and economic insecurity.

Criminal justice personnel can strengthen their role in the development of problem-specific rehabilitation programs and community based alternatives for pseudo-offenders. Probation and parole officers, along with institutional personnel, need to question the appropriateness of maintaining caseloads of "special needs" offenders. Moreover, the general public needs to register its indignation over the insensitivity of the criminal justice system to the varying needs of such persons. In fact, pressures to base criminal justice decisions on standardized approaches to offenders may run counter to the differential treatment needs of some in these groups.

Finally, jail personnel, especially social workers, must take a leadership role in monitoring intake functions for the criminal justice system. Such monitoring should promote the development of alternatives to the jail, helping to expand choices for police, courts and jail staff in both pre-trial and sentencing decisions. Hopefuly, the service innovations developed on behalf of the pseudo-offender population may offer models for more appropriate social care options for other offenders as well.

NOTES

1. Collins, P. & Deviny, K. *Jail based social services—A tale of survival.* Paper presented at the 1978 Western Society of Criminology Annual Conference, San Diego, February 1978.

2. Collins, P. & Deviny, K. *Jails are not prisons.* Paper presented at the 1978 American Society of Criminology Annual Meeting, Dallas, 1978.

3. National Coalition for Jail Reform. Position paper on pretrial release.

4. Release criteria. Used by a northwest county jail, police, and sheriff's department.

5. Hinkle, Peggy. Personal communication with caseworker for the Bureau of Developmental Disabilities, Washington State.

REFERENCES

Abramson, M.F. (1976). The criminalization of mentally disordered behavior: Possible side-effect of a new mental health law. In J. Monahan (ed.), *Community mental health and the criminal justice system*. New York: Pergamon Press.

Bentz, W.K. & Noel, R.W. (1983). The incidence of psychiatric disorder among a sample of men entering prison. *Corrective and Social Psychology, 29*, 22-28.

Briar, K.H. (1983). Jails: Neglected asylums. *Social Casework, 63*, 387-393.

Busch, E. S. (1976). Ramifications of the criminal justice system for the mentally retarded. In P.L. Browning (ed.), *Rehabilitation and the retarded offender*. Springfield: Charles C. Thomas.

Coalition for National Jail Reform. *Jail is the wrong place to be for public inebriates*. Washington, D.C.

Deheer, N. & Schweitzer, H. (1985). Suicide in jail: A comparison of two groups of suicidal inmates to jail suicide victims. *Corrective and Social Psychology, 31*, 71-76.

Ford, D. & Kerle, K. (1981). Jail standards: A different perspective. *The Prison Journal, 61*, 23-35.

Gibbons, F.X., Sawin, L.L. & Gibbons, B.N. (1979). Evaluations of mentally retarded persons: Sympathy or patronization? *American Journal of Mental Deficiency, 84*, 124-131.

Helig, S.M. (1973). Suicide in jails: A preliminary study in Los Angeles County. In B.L. Danto (ed.), *Jail house blues*. Orchard Lake, Michigan: Epic Publications.

Hudson, P. & Butts, J. (1979). Causes of death in North Carolina jails and prisons. *Popular Government, 4*, 16-17.

Jail death underscores mental health deficits. (1980, November). Seattle Times, Nov. 23, p. 22.

Jones, D.H. (1976). *The health risks of imprisonment*. Lexington, MA: Lexington Books.

Kurtz, H.A. (1981). Two years in a small Texas jail: Problems and the use of argot. *The Prison Journal, 61*, 36-42.

Miller, E.E. (1978). *Jail management*. Boston: Lexington Books.

Owens, C.E. (1980). *The mental health of black offenders*. Boston: Lexington Books.

Piliavin, I. & Briar, S. (1964). Police encounters with juveniles. *American Journal of Sociology, 70*, 206-214.

Santamour, M.B. (1986). The offender with mental retardation. *The Prison Journal, 66*, 3-17.

Santamour, M.B. & West, B. (1982). The mentally retarded offenders: Presentation of the facts and a discussion of the issues. In M.B. Santamour & Watson (eds.), *The retarded offender*. New York: Praeger Publishers, 1982.

Schwartz, V.A. (1982). A diversionary system of services for the mentally retarded offender. In M.B. Santamour & Watson (eds.), *The retarded offender*. New York: Praeger Publishers.

Steinbock, E.A. (1976). A definitional framework: Who is the retarded offender? In P.L. Browning (ed.), *Rehabilitation and the retarded offender*. Springfield: Charles C. Thomas.

Tacoma News Tribune. May 11, 1982, A-3.

U.S. Department of Justice, Bureau of Labor Statistics. (1980). *Profile of jail inmates*. Washington, D.C.: Superintendent of Documents.

Whitmer, G.E. (1980). From hospitals to jails: The fate of California's deinstitutionalized mentally ill. *Journal of Orthopsychiatry, 50*, 60-73.

Wiseman, J.P. (1971). *Stations of the lost*. Englewood Cliffs, NJ: Prentice-Hall.

Outpatient Treatment
of the Sexually Motivated Murderer
and Potential Murderer

Louis B. Schlesinger
Eugene Revitch

SUMMARY. This paper acquaints the reader with the psychopathology and psychodynamics of the sex murderer (and potential sex murderer), with an emphasis on treatment in an out-patient setting. Murder is a complex phenomenon with different clinical pictures, different etiologies and different prognoses. The authors review their system of classification based on the motivational dynamics of the act itself, and they detail the catathymic and compulsive murderer, which comprise the majority of most sexually motivated homicides. Three cases are presented that demonstrate: (1) a treatment failure due to the inability of the therapist to recognize important symptoms, (2) successful treatment of a catathymic sex murderer once released from custody and (3) successful treatment of a potential compulsive sex murderer.

In the United States today, vast resources are devoted to the apprehension, incarceration, and punishment of individuals accused and subsequently convicted of murder (including sexually motivated murder). However, little effort is expended on prevention or treatment. Although sexually motivated murders constitute a minor-

Louis B. Schlesinger, PhD, is Associate Professor of Clinical and Forensic Psychology at the University of Medicine and Dentistry of New Jersey, Newark, and Director of the Violence Clinic at the Veterans Administration Medical Center, East Orange, NJ.

Eugene Revitch, MD, is Professor of Psychiatry at the Robert Wood Johnson School of Medicine of the University of Medicine and Dentistry of New Jersey, New Brunswick.

ity of all homicidal acts, they have particularly repellent features and produce particularly tragic consequences. Therefore, serious attempts should be made to diagnose potential sexual offenders and to treat convicted sex murderers after they are released from custody. The purpose of this paper is to acquaint the reader with the psychopathology and psychodynamics of the sex murderer and to offer specific and practical suggestions for treating such individuals on an outpatient basis.

Like most psychiatric conditions, murder is not a unitary concept. There are different clinical pictures, different etiologies, different courses, and different prognoses. Clark (1971) has divided crimes (including murder) into six specific categories of social offenses. Brancale (1955) classifies them as either administrative or psychiatric; Halleck (1971) classifies them as either adaptive (motivated by some type of logic or purpose) or maladaptive (the result of psychopathology, where the motivation is not always apparent). Tanay's (1969) classification system for homicide includes (1) dissociative, (2) psychotic, and (3) ego-syntonic homicides. The ego-syntonic homicide is similar to Halleck's adaptive crime, whereas the dissociative and the psychotic correspond to Halleck's maladaptive crime. Miller and Looney (1974), in their study of adolescent homicide, argue that a significant common denominator is the degree of dehumanization of the victim by the offender. These authors believe that they can predict future violence by noting the degree of dehumanization involved in a homicidal act.

In search of a more concrete and more all-encompassing common denominator in criminal behavior, Revitch and Schlesinger have developed a classification system based on a motivational spectrum (Revitch, 1965; Revitch and Schlesinger, 1978, 1981). Acts stimulated by sociogenic or external factors are grouped at one end of the scale, and acts stimulated by psychogenic or internal factors are grouped at the other end. The system's prime purpose is to aid in solving prognostic and dispositional problems. From the exogenous to the endogenous end of the spectrum, the offenses are divided into (1) environmental or sociogenic, (2) situational, (3) impulsive, (4) catathymic, and (5) compulsive. This classification is not intended to be rigid, since borderline cases with characteristics belonging to the adjoining areas are inevitable. The exogenous factors play less and less of a role as one approaches the other extreme of the scale, occupied by the compulsive offenses. The personality variables (endogenous factors) play a lesser role in the sociogenic offenses, where environmental influences dominate.

Most cases of sex murder belong to the impulsive, catathymic, and compulsive groups, with the latter two being dominant. Acts of gynocide (the killing of women) committed by the other two groups have a strong circumstantial element and are characterized by their randomness. Repetition of the same crime is rare in the impulsive and catathymic categories and depends to a great extent on external stimuli. In the compulsive group, however, repetition of a murder is common. Some compulsive sex murderers (referred to recently as serial murderers) may struggle against the pressure to commit the act, but eventually that pressure becomes too strong and they succumb to the need.

CATATHYMIC GYNOCIDE

The term *catathymia* was introduced by the Swiss psychiatrist Hans Maier (1912), who described the condition as a psychological process or reaction activated by a strong and tenacious affect connected with a complex of ideas. Many years later, Wertham (1937) introduced the concept of "catathymic crisis" into the field of forensic psychiatry and criminal psychopathology. He used this concept to explain various unprovoked episodes of severe violence without organic etiology: "A catathymic reaction is the transformation of the stream of thought as the result of certain complexes of ideas that are charged with a strong affect, usually a wish, a fear, or an ambivalent striving" (p. 975).

The concepts of catathymia and catathymic crisis continue to appear, in various contexts, in the literature. Sedman (1966) states that catathymia implies a specific psychic vulnerability resulting from early infantile traumatization. Gayral and his colleagues (1956) describe catathymic crises ("crises catathymiques") as non-epileptic emotional paroxysms with secondary neurovegetative reactions. Revitch (1964) borrowed Gayral's concept in describing, under the name "catathymic attacks," certain seemingly unprovoked explosions of rage, with agitation and destructiveness, that he observed in a female prison population. Revitch and Schlesinger (1978, 1981) have defined catathymic crisis not as a diagnostic entity but, rather, as a psychodynamic process frequently accompanied by disorganization and characterized by an accumulation of tension released through the violent act and followed by relief. In their view (Revitch and Schlesinger, 1981), a catathymic crisis can be described as acute or chronic. The acute process is essentially a sudden, unprovoked murder or violent act without obvious motivation. Ruotolo (1968) believes that an injury to the pride system is fundamental in precipitating such rage. Satten, Menninger, and Mayman (1960) present a classic case of acute catathymic attack in their description of a soldier who — without any obvious provocation and with partial amnesia for the event — killed a preadolescent girl by drowning her.

In the chronic catathymic process, a depressed mood, loose schizophrenic-like thinking, and obsessive preoccupation may precede the violent act for weeks, months, or even a year. For some reason, the future offender comes to believe that his state of distress and tension (or his crisis) can be remedied only through an act of violence. Once that act is accomplished, the offender feels a sense of relief. In retrospect, the act itself often seems ego alien and dreamlike. Such individuals often seek treatment while they are in the incubation stage of this condition and often express ideas of violence, typically toward family members and especially toward girlfriends. As the following case illustrates, however, such revelations frequently are dismissed, and the patient is treated solely for depression — often with tragic results.

Case 1

Description. A 29-year-old male (G.W.), a salesman with a good work record and no prior involvement with the law, was undergoing therapy at the time that he murdered his second wife. His first marriage, to his childhood sweetheart, ended after one year.

About nine months before the murder, G.W. and his second wife began having serious marital difficulties. The wife threatened to divorce him, and she returned home many times to stay with her parents following an argument. Finally, she left him permanently.

After her departure, G.W. became depressed and thought about killing himself. He sought treatment at a local mental health center, but his depression did not abate despite antidepressant medication. The treating psychiatrist dismissed his ideas of violence (at this point suicide) with statements such as "There are more fish in the sea" and "You should pull yourself up by the bootstraps and get on with your life."

G.W. bought a gun and went to his wife's place of employment: "I talked to her and then I put the gun to my head and told her, 'I'm going to kill myself.' She then promised she'd come back to me." The wife brought charges against him for this incident, and G.W. served thirty days in jail "with animals" before being released on bail. He then bought another gun and again thought of suicide. Yet he maintained hope that he and his wife would reunite. With the Christmas season nearing, he began to feel worse: "I tried to contact my wife. I felt bad. People were happy but I wasn't happy. I went to see the psychiatrist at the clinic. I cried and I could feel that something was happening." He told the psychiatrist that he had begun to think about killing his wife. However, the psychiatrist erroneously believed that "he would not do it as long as he expressed himself. If he did not tell me about such a fantasy, then he would be dangerous."

The following is G.W.'s description of the events that resulted in the murder of his wife a few days after his last therapy session:

> On Christmas Eve, I decided to go to midnight mass to see my wife. I saw encouragement in her eyes. I tried to talk to her, but her mother intervened. I followed them home. I had the gun in my car. I followed them into the garage; they pulled in the garage, and I went behind them. I asked to talk to my wife. Her father hit me with a broom handle, and her mother went into the house — apparently to the call the police. I pulled out the gun. I put numerous shots into my wife. I wanted them to know I meant business. The parents were scattered. I stepped into the driver's seat and shot her in the head again and again. She fell out of the passenger side. I saw no blood on her. I said to her that I loved her, and I kissed her on the lips. Then I shot her again from close range directly in the head. I think I fired

two more shots. I walked away and felt I would throw up. I pulled the hammer back again and pointed it to my head. My hand shook so bad that I couldn't pull the trigger. I looked at her eyes and I really felt ill. I saw the police coming, so I dropped the gun. I was afraid that my father-in-law would go for it and start shooting me. I yelled at the cops to pick up the gun that I dropped.

Comment. This case provides an excellent example of a chronic catathymic process that resulted in murder; it also exemplifies a clear treatment failure. The therapist unfortunately paid no attention to G.W.'s ideas of violence and failed to recognize the depth of the inner disturbance (or, in Wertham's words, the "complex of ideas"). Instead, G.W. was treated simply for depression. The psychiatrist failed to realize that G.W.'s marital difficulties emanated from his conflictual relationship with his wife—graphically illustrated in his expression of love while killing her. The relationship had created in him a state of confusion and helplessness, and G.W. could release this catathymic tension only by eliminating the source of the tension (the victim) through homicide or by removing himself from the source through suicide. G.W. should have been hospitalized as soon as the idea of killing his wife emerged. If he had been hospitalized, the catathymic tension could in all likelihood have been released through intensive psychotherapy, at least to the extent that the current crisis was over and he would not have the pressing need to kill. The deeper sources of conflict could then have been addressed through extensive therapy on an outpatient basis.

Case 2

Description. A.B., a 27-year-old man, shot and killed his girlfriend of eight months while he was a passenger in the car she was driving. After discharging all the bullets from his handgun into her body, he left the car and ran to a phone in order to call his priest. He also intended to drive to a gun store and buy additional bullets so that he could kill himself.

The course of events leading to the tragedy probably began one year before the homicide, when he became involved with the girlfriend who preceded the victim. After six weeks of intensive dating, he became engaged to this girl. A few months later, he developed feelings of jealousy, imagining that his fiancée was dating a neighbor. He became confused and began to have doubts about the engagement and vague feelings that something was wrong. His feeling of closeness to his fiancée disappeared. During that period, he began to drink, discontinued his work on his master's thesis, and behaved in such a way that his fiancée broke the engagement. After that, he felt that his "dilemma had been solved."

A year later, while on a new job, he met the future victim and from the first encounter felt immensely attracted to her. Very soon they dated daily and within a short time decided on an official engagement. A passionate relationship was initiated and grew in intensity. For the first three months of the relationship, he felt euphoric. By the fourth month, however, he developed the same feelings that he had had during his first engagement: "I felt she was cooling off. I thought things were deteriorating." At the same time, he was extremely concerned with sex—to a point that she even asked him to change the subject. He also had vague feelings that she was disappointed in him. He continuously pressed his fiancée with questions about marriage, and at this point she apparently had second thoughts. She said that she still loved him but wanted to postpone marriage vows. His depression gradually increased in intensity, although he also had occasional feelings of euphoria.

On Christmas day, after they had exchanged gifts, he told his fiancée that they should either stop seeing each other or else should be together constantly. At the same time, he felt that his desire for her was diminishing, and "one day it entered my mind to end it all. I had continued sadness." One night he visited her and spoke about his suicide decision; she reacted with outcries of dismay. A week later, he called her on the phone and asked her whether she still loved him. In the fifth month of the relationship, a feeling of "total chaos" emerged. He described his state at the time as "functional," meaning that he performed his duties at work and elsewhere but lived like an automaton. He also developed a feeling that his fiancée was smiling at other men more than she smiled at him.

By the sixth month, he had lost about 35 pounds, and his family physician referred him to a psychiatrist. He had distinct feelings of unreality and actually failed to perceive the surroundings in three dimensions. He thought more and more about committing suicide, but "I had enough life left in me to want to live." Finally, he obtained a gun for suicidal purposes and, while thinking about suicide, fired several shots into his girlfriend's tires. On other occasions, he punctured his girlfriend's tires. He also began carrying the gun to work in his attaché case.

During the seventh month, he went to the beach one day. He called his fiancée from there and told her that he was going to shoot himself. He fired a bullet into the water and then returned home. Shortly afterward, he gave the gun to his psychiatrist, since he felt that it was not safe in his hands. He also mentioned to some acquaintances in a tavern that he was going to shoot his girlfriend, but they apparently took his comment as a joke. A week later, he returned to the psychiatrist and asked him to return the gun since he now felt better. The gun was returned, and he immediately drove to a school where, he believed, his girlfriend was taking some lessons. The school was closed, and he realized that it was the wrong day.

The idea of killing his girlfriend took such a hold on him that he was unable to cope with it. He had a feeling that "it had to be done." This idea came in spurts and then receded. In the eighth month of their relationship, he thought of contacting the mafia and paying a professional to kill his girlfriend. He also did other things that he could not explain. For instance, he called a real estate agent and recommended a friend as a client (when the friend had no interest in real estate); he also called a car dealership, saying that his girlfriend wanted to buy a car (when she did not). On one occasion, he stood on a highway with his arm extended and covered by his raincoat, in the hope that she would drive by and think he was going to shoot her.

On the night before the murder, he was in an unusually good mood. He came to work with the loaded gun in his attaché case. Throughout the day, he was intermittently depressed and elated. Thoughts of killing his fiancée alternated with thoughts of dropping the whole matter. His car was in the garage that day, and he made arrangements to be driven there after work. At the end of the workday, his obsessive preoccupation with killing his girlfriend and himself returned. She offered to take him to the garage and thus sealed her fate.

In retrospect, after the murder, the whole experience seemed to him bizarre and illogical. He could not find any motive for his act. His reasoning was so disturbed that he spoke about endowing a foundation in his girlfriend's name, although he had no income other than his salary. He said that at the time he had "an incredible inferiority complex." He believed that he was too dependent on the victim and that, in killing her, he solved two problems: (1) he achieved freedom, and (2) she would not have to live in a hostile world. Sex with her seemed to him immoral and against his religion, "like having sex with my mother."

While on parole, he was treated and followed closely over a ten-year period. He had sexual relations with various girls but avoided involvements until one young woman forced him into a steady relationship. In talking about this girl, he said: "In some way she is like my mother. My mother never said a word in rebuttal to my father. My girlfriend, although emotionally dependent the way my mother was, spoke out on issues."

No clinical evidence of psychotic manifestations could be elicited during the years of psychotherapeutic contacts. He gained insight into his major conflict and, although he knew he did not totally resolve it, felt confident that his mastery and rationality would prevent a similar outcome in the future. He eventually married, but his conflict involving intimacy remained a problem for years and he struggled with it continuously. At times, the conflict would abate and he would function rather well; at other times, it would intensify so that more frequent therapeutic sessions became necessary. He continues in treatment (after being released from prison for over ten years) and will probably need therapy for the remainder of his life.

Comment. This is a typical case of a chronic catathymic process occurring within the framework of an ego-threatening relationship. The relationship with women stimulated the unresolved oedipal conflict, which necessitated either a flight from the stimulus (suicide) or an elimination of the stimulus (homicide). Because of the diffuseness of his personality structure, A.B. could not handle the released affect. The resulting ego disintegration, obsessive preoccupations with the victim, ambivalence, and depression led him to thoughts of suicide and, ultimately, to murder. After he developed some insight about the reason for his ambivalent relationships with the opposite sex, he was able to use this insight in his continuing relationship with his current wife. In cases such as this, long-term psychotherapy has proved to be valuable.

COMPULSIVE GYNOCIDE

Compulsive murders are at the extreme endogenous end of the motivational spectrum and thus are least influenced by sociogenic factors. The individual's need to commit the act is compelling, and there is a strong potential for repetition. In some cases, the urge is so strong that the individual's attempt to resist it will bring on anxiety with somatic manifestations. Krafft-Ebing ([1886], 1934, p. 111) reported the case of a 20-year-old man who, in broad daylight, attacked young girls and stabbed them in the genitals: "For a time he succeeded in mastering his morbid craving, but this produced feelings of anxiety and a copious perspiration would break out from his entire body." William Heirens, whose career of killing women started with repetitive burglaries and the theft of female undergarments (Freeman, 1956), had headaches and profuse sweating when he resisted the urge.

Compulsive murders may be committed in a strictly ritualistic and similar manner, or the compulsive urge may be expressed in various forms but stimulated by the same dynamics. The homicides may be frequent or isolated or repeated at long intervals. Homicidal urges and fantasies may precede homicidal acts by many years, and the compulsion frequently persists after years of imprisonment.

The vast majority, but perhaps not all, of the compulsive homicides have an underlying basis of sexual conflicts. Sex murderers usually are men rather than women, and the victims usually are women. Sexually motivated sadistic murders of men by men are less common. However, some sadistic murderers may attack men, women, children, and animals. The most striking example is Peter Kurten (Wilson and Pitman, 1962), who stabbed sheep while abusing them sexually and also choked and mistreated women while courting them. Kurten sadistically murdered and mutilated women, men, and children and on one occasion killed a swan and drank its blood. The thought content of compulsive murderers includes a combination of hostility to women, preoccupation with maternal sexual conduct, overt or covert incestuous preoccupations, guilt over and rejection of sex as impure, feelings of sexual inferiority, and at times a need to possess the victim or whatever she may represent (since a lifeless body is not threatening and can be dominated).

Some individuals develop a fantasy of their mothers's purity. The maternal image is thus split into good (virtuous) mother and bad mother. In almost every case of sexually motivated gynocide, there is some unhealthy emotional involvement with the mother. The mother may be rejecting and punitive, or she may be seductive and overprotective to the point of infantilizing her son. In some cases, there is blatant sexual stimulation of the child, who may know about or have witnessed the mother's promiscuity. In all these cases, repressed incestuous feelings seem to be the main stimulus to gynocide. This type of gynocide is, in essence, a displacement of affect from the mother to other women. In other words, sexually motivated gynocide is a displaced matricide. Freud (1905, 1938, p. 572) spoke of the fusion of sex and aggression that is found in sadistic gynocide: "The sexual instinct itself may not be something simple. It may, on the contrary, be composed of many components, some of which detach themselves to form perversions. Our clinical observations thus call our attention to fusions, which have lost their expression in . . . normal behavior." There is little doubt that incestuous conflicts are the main dynamic force behind the compulsive and to a large extent even the catathymic gynocides. We have also developed a clinical impression that the more intense the homicidal compulsion, the more it is sexually motivated.

In the following case, a potential sex murderer was treated successfully on an outpatient basis and followed for a period of eight years.

Case 3

Description. On three different occasions, a 16-year-old boy broke into and entered a house located in his neighborhood. Three months after his first entry, he entered the second time; and two weeks later he entered the third time. The first entry took place under the following circumstances: Early in the evening, he cut the doorknob with a hacksaw and entered the premises while the inhabitants were out. He looked around the room and took $300, which apparently was not hidden. The second incident occurred early Sunday morning on his way to church. He found the door open. Inside, everyone was still asleep. He explored the room and found some beer on the liquor bar. After tasting the beer, he walked around the house carrying the beer bottle. He entered the bedroom of a 15-year-old girl (the homeowner's daughter) and hit her on the head with the bottle. He knew the girl from the neighborhood and school and had fantasized about her a great deal. She was apparently attractive and popular. He caused a slight injury, which needed three superficial sutures. When later interrogated by the police, he explained his actions by saying, "I guess I got some sort of thrill out of it."

The third break-in occurred in the evening. He cut the TV cable and entered the house. When asked why he did it, he said, "Just to break in." The youngest daughter of the family, however, was awake. She phoned for help, and the young man was apprehended. When his parents appeared at the police station, they found him crying. During the first entry, he also defecated on the bed (apparently in the parents' bedroom) and later telephoned the home stating "Next time you'll get pregnant."

This boy had no previous record of delinquencies. In fact, he was a mild, insecure, and compliant person who, according to his mother, was a good boy from the day of his birth. He was the youngest in the family. Although he got along with his sisters, his older brother teased him and mistreated him physically. In contrast, he was overprotected and overindulged by his mother. Until he was 16, he and his mother engaged in pillow fighting and wrestling, often damaging furniture and thereby annoying his father. The winner had to sit on the loser.

At the time of his arrest, he was in the eleventh grade at a vocational school and received good grades. He studied auto repair and was even employed part time while still in high school. After graduation, he received a steady job with a company and was highly regarded as a worker.

About two months after the last break-in, he was admitted to a psychiatric facility, on the advice of his lawyer, and was treated with individual and group psychotherapy. Two months after admission, he was discharged from the hospital against medical advice (since the staff feared that he might repeat his offenses and needed further hospitalization). He was then treated as an outpatient in individual psychotherapy. As the treatment progressed, his spontaneity increased—at first in discussion of neutral subjects, such as the school, work, and interests. Eventually, he started revealing the more intimate subjects. When he was asked whether he had engaged in voyeuristic acts, he revealed that at the age of 8 he had peeped at his sister undressing. He said that it was funny. At the age of 12, he started peeping through windows in the evenings. Whenever he saw a girl or a woman undressing, he had a triumphal feeling because "They did not see me and I saw them so I had something over them."

The three episodes of breaking and entering were connected with a feeling of depression and anger, allegedly caused by rejection from his peers. He also experienced anger during the three episodes of breaking and entering. He realized that this anger had prompted him to defecate on the bed in the master bedroom. He spoke a great deal about being physically mistreated and humiliated by his older brother without being able to retaliate. He described the victim of the assault as very popular and said that he would not attempt even to approach her because of his feelings of inadequacy and incompetence around girls. After he finished school and started work, he began going out with a group of boys and girls. By the end of two and a half years of therapy, he acquired a girlfriend and so far has not had any further trouble with the law. He eventually explained the attack on the victim as a show of courage, and he admitted to daydreams of killing or stabbing girls in the past.

Comment. In the background of this case is a seductive and overprotective mother and a dominating older brother who made him feel weak, inadequate, and shy with the opposite sex. Thus, the breaking and entering three times in the same house and finally hitting the girl on the head with a beer bottle, defecating on the bed, destroying the TV cable, and taking the $300, as well as the daydreams about stabbing girls, were basically fueled by anger and served as an "act of courage." Fenichel (1945) considers voyeurism a substitute for sadistic acting out through displacement of destructive drives by looking. Originally, this man was reserved and unable to deal with his deeper emotions and the causes of his behavior. Eventually, through therapy, he gained insight, was able to reveal his inner self (at least in sessions), improved his socialization, and even got a girlfriend. Because of certain assets—such as a good work history, an optimistic view of the future, and initial improvement—his prognosis is considered good.

SOME PRACTICAL CONSIDERATIONS IN TREATMENT

Various techniques and problems encountered in psychotherapy and pharmacotherapy with violence-prone patients have been reported elsewhere (Lion, 1972, 1975; Lion, Christopher, and Madden, 1977; Madden, 1977). We have found that it is not specific techniques that have proved helpful to clinicians but, rather, an overall plan with some practical suggestions. On the whole, the treatment of the sex murderer or the potential sex murderer should not be materially different from the treatment (by an experienced and competent clinician) of any other difficult case. Some basic and practical considerations, however, do need to be amplified.

Since there are no specific "antiviolent" drugs, just as there are no specific "antiviolent" psychotherapeutic techniques, any of the various treatment approaches might be relevant and useful in a given case. Rapport and support cannot be overemphasized. Therapeutic rapport can be problematic for many therapists because of the repellent nature of the act or of the fantasy (in the case of the potential sex murderer). Such individuals need someone whom they can connect with, someone who is available and willing to listen and provide insight at later stages of treatment. Insight is very important, but so is expression of feelings and emotions, because of the cathartic effect.

The issue of control is central in maintaining such a patient in outpatient therapy. Family members (if appropriate) should be made aware of the patient's problems. This disclosure by the therapist does not constitute a breach of confidentiality but, in fact, adds a dimension of control that is needed. Since the patient's behavior is ego dystonic, he will actually welcome such control. A thorough understanding of the Oedipal dynamics that present themselves in the context of a preoedipal structure (borderline, schizoid, or severe characterological disturbance) is also needed. Since many patients do better with additional symptom relief, medication provides added control for those individuals who act out when in states of depression, mania, or psychosis.

Unfortunately, the most experienced therapists usually do not treat such offenders—largely because of the real risk of liability (Litwack and Schlesinger, 1987). The liability problem has created a climate whereby therapists do not want to treat very disturbed or dangerous people. Legal standards that were developed to protect citizens may actually result in less protection, since practitioners— out of fear of legal entanglements—are avoiding dangerous patients, who therefore will continue their dangerous and antisocial behavior. We hope that this situation will change, so that therapists become more willing to undertake the outpatient treatment of such potentially dangerous cases.

REFERENCES

Brancale, R. Problems of classification. *National Probation and Parole Association Journal*, 1955, *1*, 118-125.

Clark, R. *Crime in America*. New York: Pocket Books, 1971.

Fenichel, O. *The psychoanalytic theory of neurosis*. New York: Norton, 1945.

Freeman, L. *Catch me before I kill more*. New York: Pocket Books, 1956.

Freud, S. Three contributions to the theory of sex (the sexual aberrations). In A. A. Brill (Ed.), *Basic Writings of Sigmund Freud*. New York: Random House, 1938. (Originally published 1905.)

Gayral, L., Millet, G., Moron, P., and Twinin, J. Crises et parocsysmes catathymiques. *Annales médico-psychologiques*, 1956, *114*, 25-50.

Halleck, S. *Psychiatry and the dilemmas of crime*. Los Angeles: University of California Press, 1971.

Kraft-Ebing, R. von. *Psychopathia sexualis*. F. J. Rebman (Trans.) New York: Physicians and Surgeons Book Co., 1934. (Originally published 1886.)

Lion, J. R. *Evaluation and management of the violent patient*. Springfield, Ill.: Thomas, 1972.

Lion, J. R. Conceptual issues and the use of drugs for the treatment of aggression in man. *Journal of Nervous and Mental Disease*, 1975, *160*, 76-82.

Lion, J. R., Christopher, R. L., and Madden, D. J. A group approach with violent outpatients. *International Journal of Group Psychotherapy*, 1977, *27*, 67-74.

Litwack, T. R., and Schlesinger, L. B. Assessing and predicting violence: Research, law and application. In I. B. Weiner and A. K. Hess (Eds.), *Handbook in forensic psychology*. New York: Wiley, 1987.

Madden, D. J. Voluntary and involuntary treatment of aggressive patients. *American Journal of Psychiatry*, 1977, *134*, 553-555.

Maier, H. W. Über katathyme Wahnbildung und Paranoia. *Zeitschrift für die gesamte Neurologie und Psychiatrie*, 1912, *13*, 555-610.

Miller, D., and Looney, J. The prediction of adolescent homicide: Episodic dyscontrol and dehumanization. *American Journal of Psychoanalysis*, 1974, *34*, 187-198.

Revitch, E. Paroxysmal manifestations of non-epileptic origin: Catathymic attacks. *Diseases of the Nervous System*, 1964, *25*, 662-669.

Revitch, E. Sex murder and the potential sex murderer. *Diseases of the Nervous System*, 1965, *26*, 640-648.

Revitch, E., and Schlesinger, L. B. Murder: Evaluation, classification, and prediction. In I. L. Kutash, S. B. Kutash, and L. B. Schlesinger (Eds.), *Violence: Perspectives on murder and aggression*. San Francisco: Jossey-Bass, 1978.

Revitch, E., and Schlesinger, L. B. *Psychopathology of homicide*. Springfield, Ill.: Thomas, 1981.

Ruotolo, A. Dynamics of sudden murder. *American Journal of Psychoanalysis*, 1968, *28*, 162-176.

Satten, J., Menninger, K. A., and Mayman, M. Murder without apparent motive: A study in personality disintegration. *American Journal of Psychiatry*, 1960, *117*, 48-53.

Sedman, G. A. A comparative study of pseudohallucinations, imagery and hallucination. *British Journal of Psychiatry*, 1966, *112*, 9-17.

Tanay, E. Psychiatric study of homicide. *American Journal of Psychiatry*, 1969, *175*, 1252-1258.

Wertham, F. The catathymic crisis: A clinical entity. *Archives of Neurology and Psychiatry*, 1937, *37*, 974-977.

Wilson, C., and Pitman, P. *Encyclopedia of murder*. New York: Putnam, 1962.